ILLUSTRATED

— (1907) —

MAURETANIA

To
My Brother
Michael
(1943–2020)

and to the skilled men of the Great
British shipbuilders of a bygone age

There is a tide in the affairs of men
Which, taken at the flood, leads on to fortune;
Omitted, all the voyage of their life
Is bound in shallows and in miseries.
On such a full sea are we now afloat,
And we must take the current when it serves,
Or lose our ventures.

(*Julius Caesar*, Act IV, William Shakespeare)

———————————

With thanks to Eric K. Longo for his valuable contributions

ILLUSTRATED

(1907)

MAURETANIA

NOTABLE EPISODES IN THE LIFE OF A LEGEND

DAVID F. HUTCHINGS

The
History
Press

UPPER DECK.

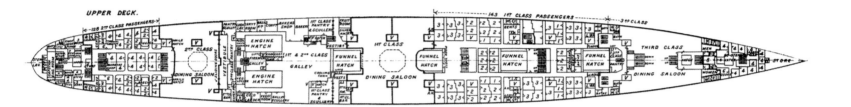

MAIN DECK.

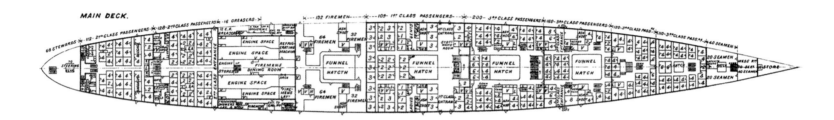

LOWER DECK.

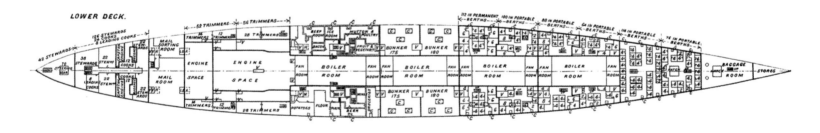

ORLOP DECK.

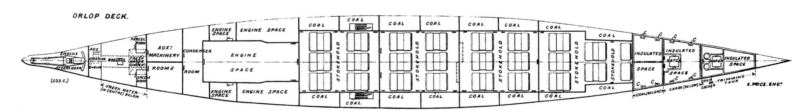

E. PRICE. ENG.

0 10 20 30 40 50   100   150   200   250   300 FEET

Cover image: Odin Rosenvinge, whose paintings graced many Cunard postcards and posters.

First published 2022

The History Press
97 St George's Place, Cheltenham,
Gloucestershire, GL50 3QB
www.thehistorypress.co.uk

British Library Cataloguing in Publication Data.
A catalogue record for this book is available from the British Library.

ISBN 978 0 7509 9715 7

Typesetting and origination by The History Press
Printed in Turkey by Imak

CONTENTS

FOREWORD BY BILL MILLER

Having been born in the post-Second World War period, in 1948, I missed seeing the *Mauretania* (1907–35) altogether. But indeed, she was one of the greatest ocean liners of the twentieth century and, like many others, I always referred to that grand four-stacker as the 'first' *Mauretania*. Her successor, another fine liner but built in 1939, was, of course, very familiar to me.

But to that first, earlier ship: she was and remains much loved, a subject of great interest, high on the list for many ship enthusiasts and collectors. For myself, I have three noted links to that Cunarder.

First, and from boyhood in the 1950s and '60s, I well remember seeing the huge model of the ship (and in white hull cruising guise) at Cunard's grand offices in Lower New York City, at 25 Broadway. It was one of those brilliant Basset Lowke models, done in the most glorious detail and fully rigged from end to end. Even in model form, the *Mauretania* looked so sleek – her raked funnels and masts, the pointed bow and, of course, the almost romantic counter stern. With its stance, the model was identical to the ship itself – reflecting power, speed, sheer ocean liner majesty and regality.

Second, on a summertime coach tour of 'all of Great Britain' in 1983, we stopped at Bristol and soon afterwards I headed for the Mauretania Pub. With the four funnels displayed in neon on the outside, I made my way indoors and there was the wood extracted from the ship itself before going to Scottish breakers in 1935. I fell almost silent. I felt I was in a 'holy place' and I felt a special closeness to the ship itself.

Third, in 2008 I was the recipient of the late Frank Braynard's collection of interior photos, large black-and-white prints, of the *Mauretania*. There were the public rooms, the promenades and foyers, and the open decks set with wicker chairs. Obtained by Frank from the company's basement archives when Cunard closed its Lower Manhattan offices in 1968, those photos remain with me, but now are increasingly facing the cruelties of old age. They are crumbling along the edges – and often crumbling quite easily.

Myself, I always enjoy reading about liners, past and present, and learning new and insightful details. But I also very much enjoy just sitting in a chair, turning the pages and looking at photographs, one after the other. Indeed, ships, long-bygone ships, come back to life. And herein, my dear friend and very competent and complete fellow author David Hutchings has brought the 'first' *Mauretania* back to life. In his latest book, what a glorious collection of photos of this grand Cunarder!

Well, the steam whistles are sounding (and screeching) again, tugs are in attendance, passengers bid their farewells and, through David's fine new book, we can sit back and see the *Mauretania* set off on another 'voyage'.

Bill Miller
Secaucus, New Jersey

ACKNOWLEDGEMENTS

The production of a book such as this relies on the kind assistance of many people, whether in the loan of precious photographs, information, or just generous encouragement.

Among these people I would again extend my very considerable thanks and deepest appreciation to Eric K. Longo for contributing so generously and so much to both the visual and informative aspects of this volume (selflessly given even as he contributed to other works). Eric's collection of contemporary correspondence from the ship's time on the River Tyne was especially invaluable in recreating the exciting atmosphere of the *Mauretania*'s launching and departures through the various correspondents' personal 'on the spot' observations.

Among others to whom I owe a great debt of gratitude (and please forgive me if I have omitted any of those kind people or organisations) who wittingly – or otherwise – have contributed, I would like to thank: Colin M. Baxter; Stephen Card; Zac Coles; Des and Ulla Cox of Snowbow/Maritime Memories for the opportunity to visit Newcastle during one of their fabulous cruises; the late John 'Jack' P. Eaton; Charles Haas; Robert Hind (the estate of John Jenkins); Nick Ireland at QinetiQ, Portsmouth (ex-Admiralty Experiment Works, Haslar); my lifelong chum and now fellow maritime author, Dick de Kerbrech; Simon Mills; Ocean Liner Enthusiasts; Ocean Liner Society; the late Peter Pearce, whose efforts saved a mass of pictorial heritage from destruction; PRC Digital of Liphook, Hampshire, for converting negatives (both glass and nitrate) and lantern slides into useable images; the estate of Captain John Pritchard; Ian Rae – especially for his expertise on the subject and for his knowledge of Newcastle and the River Tyne, the loan of many photographs, and for his personal tour of the Swan Hunter's site (now viewed only from Roman Wallsend); the enthusiast's online group RMS Mauretania Swan Hunter & Wigham Richardson, Wallsend 1907–1935; Stephen Weir, Picture Library, National Museums NI; another long-standing friend David 'Albie' Williams; and to my two lovely daughters, Emma and Alex, for believing in their Old Dad!

Most of the illustrations used are from my own collection, many obtained through that great source, eBay, and are, as such, not acknowledged. I have attempted to establish copyright of the illustrations used but, in the rare case where I have been unable to do so, I apologise to the holders. I will correct this deficiency, once established, in future editions.

At The History Press my deepest thanks go to Amy Rigg and her splendid team for believing in the project and not dismissing it as not 'just another picture book'.

And last, but no means least, my heartfelt thanks to my long-time friend Bill Miller, 'Mr Ocean Liner' himself, for writing such a generous Foreword.

To all of you – I am most sincerely and gratefully indebted.

PREFACE

When my book *RMS* Mauretania *(1907):* Queen of the Ocean was published in 2019 by The History Press, the prolific amount of text (resulting from lengthy research) led to the exclusion of many photographs that might have otherwise expanded the glorious visual story of this great liner.

As a consequence – and from kind, constructive comments received following that book's publication (such as from Dick de Kerbrech who, as an ex-marine engineer, bemoaned the lack of emphasis on the ship's most important feature, her turbines) – this current volume seeks to redress that 'shortfall'. This book is intended as an album of illustrations to further enhance various notable occurrences that befell the *Mauretania* during her long and distinguished, even legendary, career.

Every great adventure has a beginning and this 'Adventure into Adventures' seeks to illustrate but a few of the notable events (Episodes) that befell that most notable of liners – the *Mauretania*. From the conception of this, the second of the two 'New Cunarders'; her design; build; launching (the latter two 'episodes' receiving special illustrative attention); wartime as well as peacetime records; her accidents; to her incredible speed records – all are events that deserve to be regarded and celebrated and are (hopefully) represented here.

In selecting illustrations I have attempted, where the occasion has arisen (such as the ship's launching), to place several photographs together to give the image of an old flickering film of the event. I am very aware that many, oh so many, images are in existence of which I am not cognisant, but I hope that these images (some already well known but hopefully placed into sequence) will convey my enthusiasm to depict the bigger events in this great liner's career. My visual descriptions of events in the ship's life often entail the use of photographs from different periods over twenty-seven years but I hope that the reader may recall the exhortation of Shakespeare's Chorus in *King Henry the Fifth* to let 'your imaginary forces work'.

I also sincerely hope that this book will not only be seen as complementing – perhaps even supplementing – my earlier volume but also as a 'stand-alone' book that will provide those with an interest in all things related to ocean liners with a further appreciation of what goes into the making of a great ship's reputation.

I have been aided in my task by Eric K. Longo, whose help and knowledge of the ship (based on his own extensive researches, writings and collection) is, without doubt, second to none.

So the ways are greased, the champagne bottle is poised, the ocean is waiting, so let us go down the ways towards the long, adventuresome and most remarkable voyage of the most famous liner of her day – a legend that sailed into the historical annals of Britain's great maritime tradition – the *Mauretania*!

'*The most astonishing piece of marine construction in the history of oceanic navigation.*'

David F. Hutchings
Lee-on-the-Solent
Hampshire
October 2020

PRE-DESIGN: THE YEARS OF CHALLENGE (1889–1904)

In the early years of the twentieth century the British Government was worried.

For many years many ships of different nations had vied to become the fastest in the lucrative trade on the North Atlantic, with generous mail subsidies being paid for fast passages. The fastest of these ships would later be awarded the nominal Blue Ribband and shipping companies engaged in the trade competed to build the fastest of the fast. Passengers were attracted by the publicity surrounding these 'Greyhounds of the Atlantic' and there was kudos in crossing on the fastest, whether for business or pleasure, and the travellers would pay for the privilege.

The Blue Ribband passed from company to company, with British ships in the vanguard and an occasional challenge, mainly from the Americans. Two British companies, the Cunard Steamship Company and the White Star Line, were conspicuous rivals and by 1889 the latter of these two steamship lines came to the fore with their new liner *Teutonic*. She was named for the German Kaiser, who was attending a grand review of the Royal Navy in honour of his grandmother, Queen Victoria.

What attracted the Kaiser to this ship, anchored in The Solent in the company of lines of black-hulled warships, was not only her modernity and the luxuriousness of her fittings but a feature that put her one step ahead of her rivals. She had been fitted with stiffening pads under her decking so that 4.7in cannon could be quickly fitted in time of war to convert her to an Armed Merchant Cruiser (AMC). This enabled her to patrol the sea lanes that supplied Great Britain, guarding them against a potential aggressor; the speedier the ship the better she could chase a target or run from a more heavily armed warship. The Kaiser remarked to an aide, 'We must have some of these' – and have them he did.

Within a few short years the *Kaiser Wilhelm der Grosse* of the North German Lloyd (NDL) appeared – in 1897 – to be followed by three other, similar vessels and, within ten years, this quartet ruled the Atlantic with their speed. Just before their introduction into service, Cunard came out with two sisters, the *Campania* and *Lucania*, briefly taking the laurels between them before losing to the German flyers.

Shortly after the introduction of the Cunard pair and the following German competitors' entry into service, another event occurred that took marine engineering by the throat. At another gala Naval Review, again in The Solent to celebrate

Queen Victoria's Diamond Jubilee in 1897, a small private steam yacht took all those watching by surprise. The 103ft 9in *Turbinia*, designed and owned by the Honourable Charles Parsons, sped through the assembled warships at an amazing 34½ knots, easily outpacing the fast picket boats sent in pursuit.

Although powered by revolutionary turbine engines, the underlying science was not new (Archimedes' screw, windmills, watermills, etc.), the application of steam in a marine environment was. The effect that the new turbine engines had on those professionals who saw this display was not lost and soon various vessels, both military and mercantile, took advantage of the new technology. Meanwhile, the White Star Line started building a quartet of large, comfortable ships (they had given up the quest for expensive speed records) but these were powered by the now standard reciprocating engines.

But fate had not yet finished as, in 1903, the White Star Line was sold to an American combine under financier J.P. Morgan – the International Mercantile Marine (IMM) – although the British Government retained the right to use the subsidised company's ships in time of war as AMCs.

When an approach was made by the IMM to purchase Cunard, Her Majesty's Government was concerned enough to listen to Cunard's overtures to design and build two huge liners that could outpace the German threat, an expensive project that was sold to the British public as an attempt to regain the prestigious Blue Ribband and subsequently keep the company under British control.

The result would astound the world.

The Hon. Sir Charles Algernon Parsons (he was a son of the 3rd Earl of Rosse) was born in 1854 and, at the age of 30, started working for Clarke, Chapman and Co., manufacturers of marine ship engines, close to Newcastle. As head of electrical equipment development, he devised a steam turbine engine that, through his own design of a generator, could produce cheap electricity. In 1889 he left the company to form his own C.A. Parsons and Company, and also founded the Parsons Marine Steam Turbine Company in Newcastle. To demonstrate his new engine, he had a steam yacht, *Turbinia*, built, which he would use to great effect. He chose his moment carefully. His engineer daughter, Rachel, would later travel on the *Mauretania* in 1909.

The Royal Mail Ships (RMS) *Campania* (1892) and her sister *Lucania* (above, 1893) were Cunard's last great achievements of the nineteenth century. Both were built by the Fairfield Shipbuilding and Engineering Company's yard under the leadership of the progressive Sir William Pearce (he had conceived a four-funnelled, 'five-day boat' well in advance of its time). He in fact 'sold' the idea of the Blue Riband as a sales ploy to encourage British and other national shipping lines to have their ships built by his company. Built with Admiralty assistance so that they could be used in time of war, these sisters were of 12,959 gross tons and 622ft long. Both achieved the fabled yet intangible Blue Riband, having as their power unit two of the biggest triple-expansion engines built to date. (Photograph J.S. Johnston, LoC)

Making one of the most famous debuts in maritime history, *Turbinia* (104ft 9in; 44½ tons) literally burst on to the world stage when, in June 1897, this little slender-hulled steam yacht sped into view (although with the Admiralty's quiet cognisance) belching smoke, fire and steam, trailing a long, white wake behind her, during a sedate naval review that was being held in The Solent and at Spithead in honour of Queen Victoria's Diamond Jubilee (she was ensconced in Osborne House on the Isle of Wight). The yacht amply and spectacularly demonstrated the power of the new engine as she sped along at 34½ knots (39mph). Fast picket boats sent in pursuit by surprised naval officers could not catch her. Parsons' plan had worked and, within two short years, his technology was taken up firstly by the Admiralty and then by commercial shipping. (Photograph by A.J. West of G. West & Son, Southsea)

George Arbuthnot Burns, Second Baron Inverclyde of Castle Wemyss (shown in this marvellous caricature by 'Spy'), was the grandson of George Burns, one of the original partners of Samuel Cunard, the founder of the Cunard Line. It was under Lord Inverclyde's chairmanship that the two new big ships came into being, but he died on 8 October 1905 at the young age of 44 and did not see the completion of his dream.

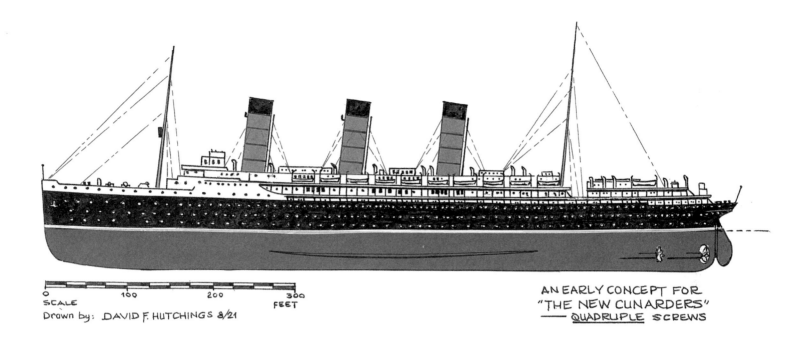

SCALE

0   100   200   300   FEET

Drawn by: DAVID F. HUTCHINGS 8/21

AN EARLY CONCEPT FOR
"THE NEW CUNARDERS"
—— QUADRUPLE SCREWS

The proposed 'New Cunarders' were planned to have six engines similar to those that had been installed on the *Campania* and *Lucania*, which, along with boilers and the all-important coal, would have taken up a massive amount of otherwise revenue-earning space. Uniquely for the time, four propellers were proposed, each, again uniquely, with four blades. The arrangement of the after two would have been problematical as they were placed either side of an aperture in the deadwood that would have originally housed a propeller had only a third been installed. This early design was transformed into a magnificent model shown at the St Louis World's Fair in 1904, where it attracted much attention and even won a medal. (Drawing by David F. Hutchings)

THE MARITIME REVOLUTION (1905-06)

In order to retain the Cunard Line as a British concern, 'Command 1703' was signed, which stipulated that the government would, under favourable terms, loan Cunard funds to construct the two planned ships, with an annual subsidy for carrying the mail, as long as they were reserved as AMCs in time of conflict. Heading the design teams were, for Cunard, Leonard Peskett, and, for the Admiralty's (on behalf of the government) interest in the ships as AMCs, Sir Philip Watts, Director of Naval Construction.

The *Mauretania* and her sister, *Lusitania*, were intended to astound and this ambition would be amply aided by the choice of engines. As originally conceived, the two New Cunarders would have required six sets of huge, space-stealing and profit-reducing reciprocating engines but, after Charles Parsons' audacious public demonstration with his *Turbinia* and following the engine's adoption in service in experimental warships, a couple of Clyde passenger steamers and two small Atlantic liners, Cunard set up a Turbine Committee in 1903 to consider its use in their new liners. Consequently the ships' designs were dramatically changed and experiments on the new hull forms were undertaken at the Admiralty Experiment Works at Haslar, Hampshire, until a final form was achieved and approved.

Fortuitously, at that time the company's hitherto largest liners (at 20,000grt), the *Caronia* and *Carmania* – the 'Pretty Sisters' – were under construction at John Brown's shipyard at Clydebank, and it was decided to delay the completion of the *Carmania* while a redesign of her after end took place to accommodate turbine engines and convert her to triple screw; *Caronia* remained powered (as designed) by reciprocating engines, and the following experiments compared the two motive powers. There had been just a half-knot difference between the sisters' top speeds but it was enough to persuade Cunard to engine their new ships with turbines. There was an increase in the *Carmania*'s running costs but these were offset by the smoother, quieter running of the ship (as well as savings in space and efficiency) and it was ascertained that comparative costs would be further reduced in the larger ships to come.

Once the basic design of the 'Express Atlantic Liners' had been tested thoroughly at Haslar, the successfully bidding shipyards (four had expressed interest) of John Brown at Clydebank and Swan Hunter & Wigham Richardson (the shipyard and engine builders had combined for the contract) at Wallsend on the River Tyne were given the ships' lines developed by Cunard and the Admiralty. Their own designers and drawing offices then set to work on preparing detailed drawings for the construction of the hulls and the building of engines. Famed designers were also tasked with the decoration of the ships and these commissions would result in some of the most spectacular rooms ever to go to sea.

After much experimentation, the dimensions of the New Cunarders were determined and, on 9 May 1904, Cunard and the Admiralty sent out tenders for a ship '760' x 87' 9" (mean shell) x 60' mld [moulded]' but both Swan Hunter & Wigham Richardson and the John Brown shipyard on the Clyde made their own recommendations for slight alterations with the result that their ship was slightly longer in overall length and had a wider beam than her erstwhile Clyde-built sister. A suggested increase of 6in of beam on the Tyne vessel was not adopted, although the same increase on her depth was.

The ship won by Swan's, Yard No. 601, was named 'Maur-*i*-tania', which fell in line with the vessel being built by John Brown's – 'Lus-*i*-tania'. However, after 'expert advice' the former's name was changed to *Maur-e-tania*.

The vital statistics for the *Mauretania* (the *Lusitania*'s differed slightly) were:

Length between perpendiculars: 760ft (both ships)

Length overall: 790ft (*Lusitania*: 785ft)

Breadth (extreme): 88ft (both)

Moulded depth 60ft (increased to 60ft 6in; 60ft 4½in for *Lusitania*)

Gross tonnage: 31,938 (*Lusitania*: 31,550)

The difference in overall lengths was a result of the *Mauretania* being given an arc of a circle as the plan for her after (poop) deck while the *Lusitania*'s was elliptical. The minimum average service speed was stipulated at 24½ knots for both.

The first plates for the keel of Yard No. 601 were laid down on the slipway of Swan Hunter & Wigham Richardson (where a special, glass-roofed gantry was erected that enabled the ship – and men – to be protected from the weather) on 18 August 1904. She would become the *Mauretania*. The *Lusitania* had been laid down at John Brown's shipyard at Clydebank a day before her Tyneside sister.

Heading the Cunard team in the design office was the company's Naval Architect, Leonard Peskett, who had been involved with the design of many Cunarders, including the *Umbria* and *Etruria*, when he was but a draughtsman, then greater involvement with the record-breakers *Campania* and *Lucania*. He led the design of the *Carpathia*, which would later find undying fame, and the 'Pretty Sisters', *Caronia* and *Carmania*, in 1905. The building of the latter was delayed so that her after arrangements could be reconfigured to enable her to be powered with turbines, thus providing a practical test bed for the acme of his achievements, the two New Cunarders. The elegant *Aquitania* followed in 1914 and would be the longest lived of all the four-funnelled liners. Leonard Peskett died in March 1924.

Looking after the Admiralty's interests in the design was Peskett's opposite number, Sir Philip Watts, who been appointed Director of Naval Construction in 1902. Sir Philip, a brilliant naval architect, had – as a shipwright apprentice – been educated at the Dockyard School in Portsmouth (as was Leonard Peskett) before moving to further his studies at the Royal School of Naval Architecture in South Kensington, London. He eventually, as a member of the Royal Corps of Naval Constructors, became Chief Constructor before moving on to Armstrong Whitworth & Co. at Elswick, where he oversaw the design and build of warships, many for foreign navies. Returning to the Admiralty in 1902, he soon became involved with the design of the New Cunarders. Sir Philip died in 1926.

The building of the *Carmania* – one of the two 'Pretty Sisters' – was delayed so that her engine room and propeller arrangement could be adapted to incorporate turbine machinery. Her sister, *Caronia*, remained as a reciprocating-engined vessel so that a comparison could be made between the two forms of engine. (Collection of Chris Mason)

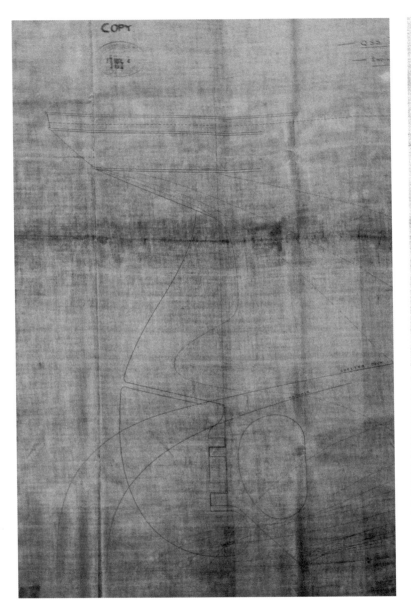

A guidance drawing produced by the Admiralty Experiment Works at Haslar of one proposed arrangement of the stern. Various models were made and tested in the Works' Towing Tank under the superintendency of Robert Edmund Froude, the son of the instigator of model testing and the founder of the tank, William Froude. (QinetiQ/Author's collection)

Model OM. Vickers Maxim design; 760' × 78' × 32·5'(mean), displt 36,010 tons (naked); full size. Lines received 24 Jan. '03. Model tried at three different draughts.

Model ON. Swan and Hunter design; 760' × 80·3' × 32·5'; displt 36,760 tons (naked); Scale ⅟₄₈ full size. Lines recd. 28 Jan. '03. Model tried at three different draughts.

Model OO. Foregoing fined to reduce displt by 1000 tons. Modification laid off at Haslar. Model tried at departure draught only.

Model OQ. Brown & Co's design; 725' × 80' × 33·5'; displt 35,400 tons (naked). Scale ⅟₄₇ full size. Lines recd. 14 Feb. '03. Model tried at two different draughts.

Sheet 10; shews the E.H.P. curves from OM; also, in this case, Fall of Ends.

Sheet 11; shews do. from ON and OO.

Sheet 12; shews do. from OQ.

IV. Experimental Forms.

[Both these, also, usual model finish, &c. as above; for body plans see Sheet 2, and for curves of areas &c, Sheet 18.].

Model OR. 760' × 85' × 32·5' (loaded draught); displt 36,500 tons (naked); Scale ⅟₄₈ full size. Lines laid off at Haslar to give the above dimensions, and a displt not exceeding 36,500 tons; according to instructions of 13 and 17 Feb. '03.

A page from a letter-book kept at the Admiralty Experiment Works at Haslar of reports sent to the Admiralty's Royal Corps of Naval Constructors. This page shows that the hulls of two previous record-breakers, the remarkable Inman liner *City of Paris* (1889) and Cunard's own *Campania* (1892), were considered good enough to serve as patterns for the New Cunarders'. Submissions were invited from several shipyards and, from the three referred to on this page, the proposal of a vessel 760ft between perpendiculars (the favoured length) from Vickers Maxim was rejected because the submitted beam of 78ft was insufficient. This yard withdrew from the tendering because 78ft was the maximum beam that could be manoeuvred through its dock gates. (QinetiQ, Haslar)

Test models at Haslar were made from paraffin wax that was roughly cast before the hull was shaped in steps using trammel cutters then finely finished using hand-held scrapers and templates. The model's form was checked carefully with templates during its manufacture.

To test their version(s) of the design, Swan Hunter & Wigham Richardson built a large, 1/16-scale, electrically propelled model using a double thickness of beautiful yellow pine, which easily enabled the moulding-in of any alterations to bow and stern lines. The model had various functions, not the least of which was to test the size and position of the propellers. For the very first time the New Cunarders were incorporating four propellers (three had only very recently been introduced into ship design) and their precise positioning was essential as the turbulence from the forward pair had an unknown effect on the after set. The Swan Hunter & Wigham Richardson model, operated by two men, was manoeuvred up and down the 24ft-deep Northumberland Dock in dozens of experiments to test bow and stern forms as well as placements of propellers.

A.   ELECTRIC MOTORS
B & B'   MOTOR AND GEAR FOR DRIVING INDICATING DRUMS
C & D   DRUMS AND INDICATING GEAR FOR TORQUE DIAGRAMS
E.   TORQUE DYNAMOMETER
F.   BRAKE PULLEY
G.   TACHOMETER
H.   THRUST BLOCK
I.   BALANCE INDICATING THRUST

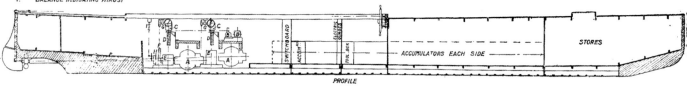

PROFILE

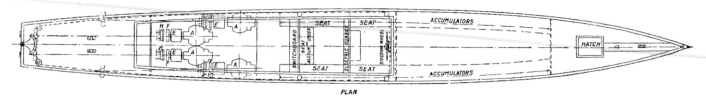

PLAN

Fig. 9.—Electric Launch.

After much thorough thought, calculation and experiment line plans (the profile, plan and body plan that showed the curvature of the ship at evenly spaced sections) were finalised by naval architects, draughtsmen and other specialised technicians. The general arrangement of the ship was prepared, as was a rigging plan that showed rivet positions. Half-block models were made on which to draw plate positions and, once all aspects of the design were complete, draughtsmen (chief, senior, leading, ordinary and apprentice) prepared detailed drawings for all parts of the ship's construction in drawing offices specialising in hull, engine and electrical engineering. The tools of the draughtsmen included: drawing benches; ruler; slide rules (or a 'Fuller's') for calculations; scale rules; French and railway curves; compasses; dividers; pencils; pens; India ink; splines; weights; essential India-rubber erasers; etc. Drawings were then sent to lady tracers, whose hand-printing was to a high standard. Copies of drawings were then printed either on paper or linen for distribution to the various departments and shops within the shipyard after being approved by the on-site Admiralty Surveyor. Silence generally ruled in these environments, with due deference being shown to those in charge. The bowler hat placed on the front drawing board denoted the authority of the Chief Draughtsman. (*Engineering*)

EPISODE 3

THE BUILDING OF A LEGEND

The date 18 August 1904 was a red-letter day on Tyneside as it saw the first keel plate of Yard No. 735 ordered under Contract No. 601 being laid on the slipway of No. 1 (covered-in) Berth beneath the specially constructed, glass-roofed building gantry. This, in itself, was an innovation as a ship was usually built on a slip open to the elements, each piece being added to the whole in all weathers. To this initial plate others were gradually added fore and aft, their touching edges joined by butt straps with three rows of rivets on each side of the join. On top of this a second plate was placed and then a third, giving a greater thickness of steel that formed the outer keel. Along the centreline of these plates a vertical plate (the vertical keel) was erected and on top of this two more thicknesses of plate were laid to form an inner keel.

The outer and inner keels were extended outwards to form outer and inner bottoms and, between these, two sets of vertical 'walls' were erected; transverse floors and fore-and-aft longitudinals divided the double bottom into a cellular arrangement, with manholes cut to provide access and inter-compartment flooding except where watertight integrity was required (i.e. in way of bulkheads). The resulting 'honeycomb' provided storage for water, both ballast and potable, and later for oil storage, for which the ship had been potentially designed should ever the price and availability of

oil warrant a conversion. The double bottom also provided a bastion against flooding in the event of damage being sustained to the outer bottom. A horizontal margin plate was attached to the outer junction of inner and outer bottoms, on to which brackets were riveted to provide a base for the local frame. The spacings of these decreased as the hull narrowed towards bow and stern. Knees (brackets) were attached to the frames, on to which transverse beams were attached, these forming the 'joists' for decks. Once the frames were in place, the external shell plating of the ship could be erected and riveted into place, the sound of which was, at the time, the signature tune of any shipyard.

Extra thicknesses of plate were incorporated into the 'Tank top' – the inner bottom – in way of engines and boilers as additional load-bearing strength was necessarily required in these areas. The decking in the boiler rooms was also susceptible to corrosion created during the working of these rooms (chemical reactions resulting from water, coal, etc.).

Any structural change that was thought necessary during construction needed official approval, and E.W. de Russett (Swan's Naval Architect) would write to the Admiralty, Cunard and the classification society Lloyd's Register of London, represented at the shipyard by its surveyor, Mr Champness, to discuss proposed changes to the original drawings (the general arrangement of the ship's layout was considered to be inviolate). Hundreds of such letters, often accompanied by drawings showing the proposed changes, were exchanged during the course of the build, especially during 1904 when the design was being finalised.

An important change to the design suggested by Mr de Russett was to use high-tensile steel (HTS) in several places on the ship, especially at the almost right-angled junction of side and deck plating along the Shelter Deck – the major uppermost strength deck before the superstructure. This alteration had the double advantage of saving weight, as HTS plates of a lesser thickness than mild steel could be used, and of providing extra strength.

Gradually, over many months, the ship's construction continued until the vessel was externally complete but as yet without funnels, ventilators, masts and other distinctive fittings. Four three-bladed propellers manufactured in London at Messrs Stone's foundry in Hope Anchor Lane had been fitted towards the end of construction (to avoid damage) and were a major distinguishing feature of the ship as her stern pointed riverwards. Internally she was almost an empty shell other than for her engines, with bare pillars and bulkheads indicating rooms where fine woodwork would later be fitted.

She was now ready for what would be the first of perhaps many dangerous journeys in her life – her launching.

To facilitate the building of Yard No. 735, an enormous double steel and glass-roofed gantry was constructed by the yard's own workforce at the western end of the old Wallsend yard that would enable work to be carried out in all weathers. The building slips beneath the gantry were named A- and B-Berths. A railway branch line served the various workshops that were also located nearby.

Clockwise from top left: Charles Sheridan Swan had taken over the management of the shipyard on the Tyne that had been owned by his brother-in-law, Charles Mitchell, but met an untimely death aged only 48. While returning from a business trip to the Continent, he fell overboard from the cross-Channel ferry *France* in April 1879 and was killed by one of the paddle wheels. His widow maintained the business until eventually entering into a partnership with George Hunter, the yard being renamed C.S. Swan & Hunter.

At the age of 13, George Burton Hunter spent two years in a civil engineer's office before becoming articled to a shipbuilder in Sunderland. A move to Clydebank in 1869 saw him working for Robert Napier and Sons, the renowned shipbuilders and marine engineers, whose many achievements had previously included building the engines for the first four Cunard paddle steamers and later building and engineering other ships for Cunard. Napiers fell into financial difficulties so, in 1873, Hunter returned to Wearside. When his partnership there with S.P. Austin (Austin and Hunter) was dissolved in 1879, Hunter joined forces with the widow of C.S. Swan and became manager of a new Tyneside firm, C.S. Swan & Hunter. By 1893 the yard was the largest shipbuilder on Tyneside and, in 1895, Hunter became its chairman. To enable a bid for one of the contracts to build one of the New Cunarders, Swan Hunters joined forces with adjacent engine builders Wigham Richardson, thus forming Swan Hunter & Wigham Richardson. The combined crowning glory, Yard No. 735, would become legendary as 'The Pride of the Tyne'.

A devout Quaker, John Wigham Richardson had been apprenticed to a paddle and screw tug builder at Gateshead. Later he would find work as a marine engine draughtsman. In 1860, at the age of 23, Richardson purchased a shipyard on the Tyne, which he named, appropriately, Wigham Richardson. The new business included engine and shipbuilding works – the latter including the Neptune Yard at Walker, which became not only the oldest on the Tyne but one of the last to be closed in the late twentieth century (entertainer Jimmy Nail sang 'The Neptune Yard was the last to go' in his poignant 'Big River'). In 1903 Wigham Richardson joined forces with Swan Hunter in order to bid for the contract to build one of the New Cunarders. Known locally as 'the great combine', Swan Hunter & Wigham Richardson immediately became one of Britain's largest and finest shipbuilders.

Andrew Laing was one of those remarkable people that history occasionally thrusts into the limelight of the stage of engineering by showcasing ability, inventiveness and determination – qualities that led to Great Britain becoming the greatest shipbuilding country in the world. By Andrew Laing's efforts, the speed of successive ships gradually increased and the list of his triumphs includes many record-breakers – *Arizona* (a speedster that was famed for surviving a head-on collision with an iceberg); *Alaska*; *Etruria*; *Umbria* (the last two having sails in case the single screw should malfunction); *Campania* and *Lucania*; as well as the slower *Ivernia* (her huge funnel gave her the epithet of 'The Ship on Stick'!); and the plucky little *Carpathia*. It was estimated that his engines reduced the time spent in crossing the North Atlantic by over a day, the resultant savings and prestige in owning a fast ship more than encouraging owners to place orders in his yard. Andrew Laing's 'mechanical genius' reached its zenith with the six great turbines that would propel Yard No. 735.

A rivet boy tends his furnace with foot-controlled bellows. There were several types of rivet used in the construction of the *Mauretania*, the principal two used in the hull being snap- or round-headed, and countersunk. The rivets would be heated to a carefully judged colour before being tossed (using tongs!) to a catcher, who caught the fixing in a bucket before placing the hot rivet into a prepared hole. The catcher then kept the rivet pushed into its location with a dolly (a lump of steel, perhaps an old sledgehammer head) before two men with sledgehammers alternately dealt the exposed shank of the rivet several skilfully precise blows, shaping it into a neat dome. On cooling, the rivet shrank tightly, pulling the two plates together. (J.I. Thornycroft)

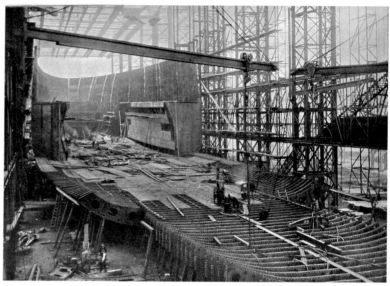

The boilers and turbines that would hopefully push No. 735 along at record speeds were mounted atop the ship's inner bottom, the Tank top. The illustration above shows the progress of build where the inner-bottom plates are being laid and the forward framing has been erected. Coal bunkers that would double up to help protect the boiler rooms are well advanced on either side, and margin plates atop the tank spaces are being laid. Note the horseshoe shape of the hydraulic riveting machines to the right and left (bottom). These machines were used in straight areas of plating. Hand riveting was utilised where plates had curvature and smoke from rivet furnaces can be seen towards the bow. Photograph taken on 18 April 1905. (*Engineering*)

The hull plating is shown here as almost complete except for the uppermost strakes. It appears from this impressive photograph that tubular scaffolding has been utilised in lieu of trimmed tree trunks that were previously used and must have been one of the first instances of its use, having only been developed by Daniel Palmer Jones and David Henry Jones at the turn of the century.

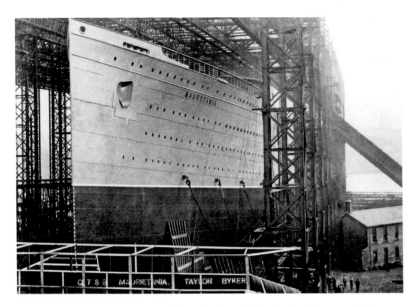

With the River Tyne gleaming through the mist in the background, this unusual photograph by Taylor of Byker shows the *Mauretania* almost ready for launching. The platform below her forefoot for the invited guests is almost complete, with bunting already in place, and the attachments for the drag chains can clearly be seen just above the waterline, while the bow-supporting fore poppet (cradle) keeps the bulk of the hull steady. An impression of scale can be determined from the workmen walking in the lower foreground (right). (Collection of Eric K. Longo)

Painted grey on the orders of George Hunter (to better show the hull in press photographs), the *Mauretania* sits proudly on the ways, her propeller edges protected against damage and painted white to impress. On the right of the gentleman peering over the stern is the chimney to a temporary boiler used to produce steam for on-board equipment required during and after launching. Another such boiler was sited on the fo'c'sle. (From a glass lantern slide.)

THE TURBINE REVOLUTION

As the ship's hull was being constructed on the ways of the shipyard, so the turbines were being built in the engine department of Wigham Richardson's works under the direction of that 'mechanical genius', Andrew Laing.

There would be six huge turbines installed in the ship – two high-pressure and two low-pressure turbines and, because these four could only operate to drive the ship forward (geared turbines were yet a thing of the future), two astern turbines. As previously mentioned, the original intention for the two ships was to install six huge reciprocating engines that would have taken up a vast amount of space, extending upwards through three – even four – decks, thus taking away valuable revenue-earning space that could have been use for cargo or passengers. Together it was planned that the turbines would produce 60,000shp (shaft horsepower) to give the ships a contract speed of 24½ knots.

Each turbine consisted of a casing that was cast in two parts (each part in sections) – upper and lower – their inner faces lined with static blades (stators) that would direct steam on to a rotor fitted with thousands of turbine blades individually placed by hand. Each rotor consisted of various stages with diameters increasing away from the steam inlet. This was to enable the steam that lost pressure as it expanded to maintain its power as it progressed down the length of the rotor and thus to the propeller shaft.

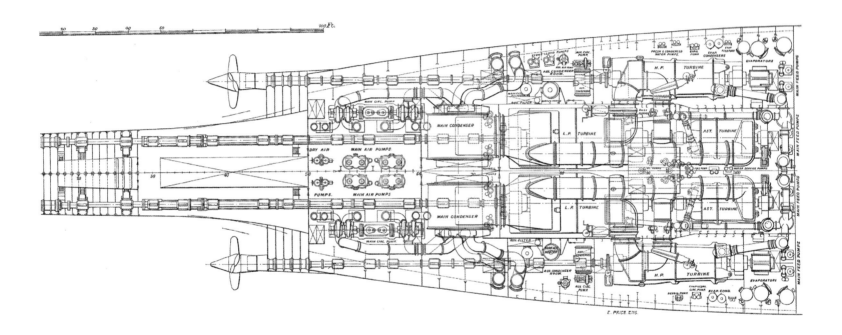

A plan of the Turbine Engine Room. (*Engineering*, 8 November 1907)

In a dust-free area, a fitter 'blades up' a turbine ring of a small diameter. This was probably destined for one of the four turbo-generators each of 375kW supplying a total of 16,000A at 110v at 1,200rpm. Among other functions, the electrical supply lit 6,000 light bulbs – a luxury at a time when most households were lit by gaslight, oil lamp or even candle.

A bladed, larger-diameter segment of up-to-date turbine technology is displayed proudly ...

... before it joins its companions to form a complete ring. Sets of rings would then be fitted into ...

... a rotor, which formed the core of one of two high-pressure (HP) turbines, seen here finished after being turned in a lathe and fashioned with grooves in readiness to take scores of rings, or of two low-pressure (LP) turbines. The changes in the diameters of the various stages increased away from the steam inlet (to account for the loss in steam pressure), the overall taper of the HP turbines being much less than that of the LP set. The 'honey dipper' to the left of the shaft was destined to sit in a block with corresponding grooves to create a thrust block that would change the rotation of the shaft into the thrust required to push the ship ahead at, hopefully, the stipulated speed of 24½ knots.

A Parsons LP, direct-acting turbine sits between its upper and lower casings in readiness to be closed and bolted together. The LP had five stages of expansion, while the HP had eight. There were also two HP astern turbines that operated the inboard (aftmost) shafts only. As built, the engines produced a total of 68,000shp but, later, 76,000shp was made on a record run. Although the ship would be launched with the turbines in situ, the piping, which would feed steam from the boilers to the turbines, would be fitted during fitting out – some of a huge 72in diameter, testament to master coppersmiths skilled in their craft. The complex arrangement of other pipes feeding the lifeblood of steam to the turbines gave an impression of some monstrous, inanimate creature on life support (reciprocating engines had much external visual movement – and resulting vibration). Four smaller turbo-generators each of 375kW supplied a total of 16,000A at 110v at 1,200rpm.

No. 3 of the four boiler rooms (stokeholds) is illustrated. The boilers were lowered into the ship by the floating crane *Titan* during the fitting-out period as the ship lay alongside as they would have greatly increased the hull weight during the launching. (*Engineering*)

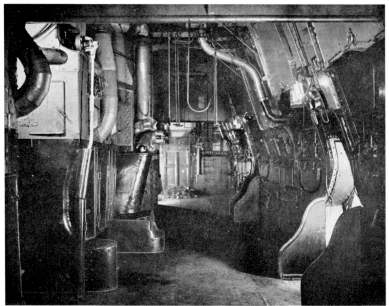

Sitting on a small railway bogey in the Boiler Shop, a boiler front with four furnaces awaits fitting into a drum. There were twenty-three double-ended and two single-ended boilers with a total of 192 furnaces, arranged in four boiler rooms protected on each side (as per Admiralty practice) by longitudinal bulkheads that also formed the inboard bulkheads to the coal bunkers, providing a protection to the boiler spaces from anticipated shellfire. (*Engineering*)

The 'naked' propeller boss. Three bronze blades would be attached to each of the four massively engineered bosses via heavy-duty steel bolts. But, because of dissimilar metal combinations, this infrequently caused problems that led to a lost blade during a crossing.

When having a photograph taken was still a novelty, a group of very proud shipwrights pose by the port aft supporting poppet. Their memories of building and launching 'The Pride of the Tyne' would be zealously passed down from generation to generation.

EPISODE 5

20 SEPTEMBER 1906

The day chosen for the launch of the *Mauretania* was Thursday, 20 September. That dying day of Summer had started off cloudy and wet but 'in the afternoon the sun shone out, and the air was quite warm'. The temperature reportedly reached 64°F (18°C). For several hours before the launching of the largest liner in the world a great crowd arrived, people flocking in their thousands from near and far by foot, tram and by rail, and gathering at various vantage points, finding 'every conceivable spot … even the ends of the Staithes' from which to witness the event. The ballast hills (heaps of stones unloaded from arriving coal ships) at Hebburn, opposite the shipyard, proved to be a specially popular site, with temporary seats being available at 1*s* (proceeds going to the Hebburn Infirmary), their occupants being entertained by 'acrobats, tricksters, and musicians'. 'Betty' wrote to her sister, saying that she 'had never seen such a sight in her life' as both sides of the river became blackened with humanity and the river itself became busy with 'every kind of boat in Christendom'. Getting to Newcastle itself was not without its tragedy as a rail accident had proven fatal to one hopeful spectator travelling up from London.

Local shipyards had issued tickets for their premises to be used as grandstands and the Corporation Quay became a popular spot. Swan Hunter & Wigham Richardson had sent over two 200 lavishly printed invitations to distinguished guests who would crowd the ribbon-decked VIP platform specially built at the forefoot of the ship. The shipyard had also distributed hundreds of tickets to the families of the workforce who could enter the yard as spectators from 3.30 p.m.

The morning of the launch had been occupied by the ship's sponsor, the comfortably be-furred Dowager Duchess of Roxburgh, touring both shipyard and engine works while ensconced in the lead motorcar of a VIP cavalcade, before being entertained at a luncheon (and the attendant speeches) prior to the 'main event'.

Much necessary work had been required to ready the mighty vessel for her launching, including huge bundles of old chains being piled along the forward areas of the slipway floor, six each side of the hull and connected to the ship by cables. These drag chains would be activated by the movement of the ship after starting her backslide to the water, their purpose to check the ship's speed and help to bring her to a halt once she reached a calculated point in the river, thus preventing her from ramming the opposite bank.

Originally it had been anticipated that Queen Alexandra would launch the *Mauretania* during a royal visit to Newcastle in July 1906 but the vessel had not been ready in time. Perhaps just as well as, although Their Majesties had been lavishly received in the city, the weather had been precociously inclement! Had the Queen been able to do so, she would have completed a family double act in launchings for that year (a royal event rare in itself) as her husband, King Edward VII, had been in Portsmouth in February to launch another revolution in shipbuilding – HMS *Dreadnought*. Not only was this the first major warship to be powered by turbines (she had been model tested in the tank at Haslar, as had the New Cunarders) but, with her standardisation of armament, she rendered all other battleships in the world obsolete (including those of Great Britain itself). Her launch thus started a great naval race with Germany that would see its culmination in the as-yet unforeseen Great War.

The launching of the *Mauretania* had been scheduled for the mid-afternoon flood tide and, about forty-five minutes prior to the event, a gang of Shipwrights started to knock away the shores supporting the great vessel, the heavy baulks of timber falling to the earth or crashing on top of those already fallen.

A procession of distinguished guests had steadily arrived, trudging their way to the launching platform through the dust of the shipyard and, when all were assembled, the Duchess of Roxburgh entered, elegantly escorted up the approach ramp by G.B. Hunter, Chairman of Swan Hunter & Wigham Richardson, resplendent in silk top hat and frock coat.

It is without apology that so many illustrations of the launching have been included for this major episode.

The boss from p. 37, now with blades affixed. The high speed of the shafts (198rpm) taken from the direct-acting (ungeared) turbines would soon create additional problems with this outmoded system.

A caravan of open motor cars carrying several VIP guests, including the *Mauretania*'s sponsor, the Dowager Duchess of Roxburgh, in the white fur collar, were (hopefully) thrillingly driven through a tunnel of funnels laid end to end in the shipyard, the guests posing for the camera as they emerged from the unique experience! The party then proceeded to inspect the huge turbines (one suspects with bemusement at what they were being shown) in the Point Pleasant works of the Wallsend Slipway & Engineering Company. The expense that these inspections incurred could not have been inconsiderable! These privileged guests were then entertained to luncheon.

Crowds of eager spectators began to gather from an early hour and soon covered every available vantage point. This incredible photograph shows Ballast Hill at Hebburn, opposite the shipyard, as people started to assemble to watch the launching. In the early twentieth century, people donned their 'Sunday best' for special events and many ladies wore their best white, fashionably figure-hugging Edwardian dresses for the occasion, while older women (strolling in foreground) still wore their full Victorian black skirts, short cloaks and bonnets. The hill would soon be completely covered with a pyramid of humanity. (Paul Perry Collection)

As tens of thousands gathered on shore, so others took to the water on dozens of pleasure craft until the river was dense with vessels jockeying for the best position. A vast array of these small craft all but obscured the silhouette of distant Hebburn, the spectators aboard loading them 'like Norwegian timber boats' with 'passengers seem[ing] to be hanging to ... funnel[s] and to the sides of the wheelhouse'. (Collection of Eric K. Longo)

Normally the preside of shipyard workers, the slipway is invaded by the curious public as men, women and children clamber over timbers and other hazards around the ship in a last-minute chance to inspect.

To the west of the slipway, other spectators populated the ferry wharf that provided them with a view of the launching that would happen just a few yards away. The ship herself, with her propellers painted white for the occasion, seems to be like a racehorse straining at the starting post.

The ticket-holding public was exhorted to begin entering the shipyard from 3 p.m. and many of these had a vantage point to the east of the slipway. In one of a series of rare views, people eagerly await the time of launch, while a paddle tug also awaits her call to duty to aid the ship once she is afloat. Spectators in their Sunday best of large picture hats for the ladies and starched collars for the small boys wait in silent, almost reverent, patience for the big moment.

Moments before the launching, a gang of shipwrights knocks away supporting shores, leaving the ship on the ways supported only by the fore poppets.

The VIP guests trudge along a roped off walkway (to keep the workers and ordinary spectators out, no doubt) between ship and railway track towards the substantially built, flag-bedecked launch platform. Workmen mill around under the ship's bow and a band plays airs in the bandstand to the left. On reaching the summit ... (Courtesy Richard Smye)

... the richly attired VIPs crowd on to the special grandstand. Among the throng were representatives of the Cunard Board and the designers, the Admiralty, Members of Parliament, members of the nobility, the clergy, etc. A top-hatted George Hunter can be seen towards the front (right, off centre) with his hands on the railing. To his left stands the Dowager Duchess of Roxburgh. Beneath the platform lesser mortals – workmen and their families – await the big moment.

Mid-afternoon and 'About 3.45 we heard the hammering' as teams of shipwrights, reportedly singing a 'chanty', began knocking away the shores – baulks of timber that supported the hull. Between the noise of this and the actual launch, a 'great silence' descended over the whole area, broken only by the occasional sound of 'hammer on wood' and 'people coughed as if they were in church'. Then the yard buzzer sounded to announce that the launch was imminent; the band ensconced to the starboard side of the ship's bow struck up. 'Every one was on the tiptoe of excitement in fact held their breath ...' A quarter of an hour later the liner was christened by the Dowager Duchess of Roxburgh, who named the ship 'with appropriate gracefulness' as she sent a bottle of champagne to its frothy destruction embellished with ribbons of red, white and blue and a specially woven golden ribbon embroidered with the ship's name and details of the special day.

As the eight 4¼ft × 4ft iron triggers that held her in place were released and the ship began her natal journey, the band struck up a tune, 'Mauretania', specially composed for the occasion by local composer Robert Saint. This tune would be played thirty-two years later at the launch of another *Mauretania* and, in more recent memory, during HM The Queen's exit at the 2016 Trooping of the Colour.

All eyes were fixed on the great, 16,800-ton hull and, as soon as it started to move, 'the shout went up "she's moving"' and 'a cheer burst from every throat' as the *Mauretania* slipped easily – to the untrained eye – down the slip and into the Tyne and 'oh! the roar of voices, whistles, buzzers until she reached the water was deafening ... one of the grandest sights ever seen'. At the ship's launch, representing the culmination of years of planning and careful calculation, the *Mauretania* sped on her way with 290.5cwt of tallow mixed with 22cwt of soft soap and 12.5cwt train oil spread between ground (static) ways and sliding ways. Halfway down the slip, which had a declivity of 1-in-24 (½in-in-1ft), the ship's motion activated the first of the huge bundles of drag chains destined to slow and then halt the vessel's backward progress to prevent her from hitting the opposite shore. The chains' sudden awakening caused clouds of rust dust to rise into the air that combined with the smoke created by the friction of the hull on the greased launch-ways. Workers waved their caps (lower left) as an early motion-picture camera crew (seen on a high platform in the gantry in the right-hand corner of this action-packed photograph) hand-cranked their machine to record the drama of the moment.

As she emerges from the protecting cocoon of the building gantry and enters the water, her bows are still on dry land and her stern is, in effect, afloat in the water. At this critical moment downward and upward forces vie with each other as the bow pushes downwards with a calculated force of 3,700 tons while the now buoyant stern is lifted. A great downward strain is now placed on the fore poppets. Cables holding the twelve bundles of drag chains (1,015 tons in total) tauten under great strain (the first was activated after the hull had travelled 33ft down the slip) and, as planned, bring the hull to a halt to within 2ft of a calculated position of arrest. The ship had moved 951ft during her birth throes.

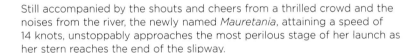

Still accompanied by the shouts and cheers from a thrilled crowd and the noises from the river, the newly named *Mauretania*, attaining a speed of 14 knots, unstoppably approaches the most perilous stage of her launch as her stern reaches the end of the slipway.

During that backward rush into the river, great timbers from the sliding ways were thrown into the air to within a few yards of the crowded pier where the Wallsend and Hebburn Direct Ferry's landing stage was acting as the Corporation grandstand. The timbers would be salvaged for future use.

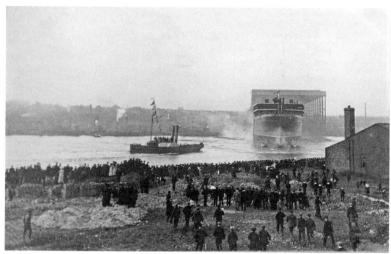

The momentum of the launching is brought to check by the twelve bundles of drag chains temporarily attached to the ship's plating by gradually released cables, the last bundle being activated into sudden motion when the ship's bow was 87ft from the end of the ways. The great hull dramatically – and undoubtedly to the excitement and perhaps with not a little apprehension on the part of the spectators on the opposite side of the river – seemed to magically stop when 222ft from the Hebburn side, coming to a halt only 5ft after the last bundle had been jerked into rusty dusty action. Mathematics and physics had worked their magic!

As the ship is finally brought to rest after seventy seconds of movement, the once-taut drag cables seem to thankfully sag as their vital roles are relinquished. Tugs-in-waiting rush up to take towing lines from the ship prior to the *Mauretania* being escorted to her fitting-out berth only a few hundred feet away between the Middle and East Yards.

Safely in the Tyne, the *Mauretania*, bedecked with celebratory flags undulating over her upper deck, makes a connection with an attendant tug at her stern. Shortly afterwards vessels carrying hundreds of spectators close in on the newly launched ship, their memories of this special day to remain with them and, through its telling, with their families for generations to come.

Those watching from ashore were eager to share the spectacle of the ship being towed to her fitting-out berth, but 'Within a very few minutes the volume of smoke from the now moving steamers almost completely hid her from view. Truly she had found her birthplace in the Smoky Tyne!'

At Waalsend ther's a greet big ship
Myad by th' great combine, man
It beats them sail just tyek ma tip
A liner fast an fine, man.
Its length is nigh eight-hundred feet
Its speed ther's nyen afloat can beat.
Its champion o' th' great Cunard fleet
An' built upon the Tyne, man.

She'll carry owre three-thoosand folks
Across the briny main, man,
An gan alang wi' pooerful strokes
Just like a railway train, man.
Nigh thorty-thoosand plates o'steel –
The figures myek wor poor heeds reel –
But it's a triumph as can feel
Ov Tyneside hands an' brain, man ...

Part of a poem composed in 'Geordie' dialect by 'J.E.S.' to celebrate the day. The latter part is not quoted as it 'cocked-a-snoop' at the Germans and their Kaiser now that their maritime superiority of many years on the North Atlantic had been vanquished into second place by the day's launching. Following the ceremony, the VIPs took tea in the Mould Loft, accompanied by traditionally enthusiastic (sometimes overly so) speeches of mutual congratulation between builders and contractor.

EPISODE 6

FITTING OUT, FITTINGS AND FEATURES

The newly launched, as-yet funnel-less *Mauretania* – 'the long, splendidly modelled steamer' – was towed to her fitting-out berth consisting of two specially built dolphins (piled structures) set away from the river wall of the yard. Access to the ship would be via a substantial steel gangway over which hundreds of workmen would cross every day to practise their trades and crafts in turning the steel hull into a luxurious ocean-going liner.

The men's tasks were prodigious. Twenty-seven boilers had to be lowered into the ship one by one, and engine rooms had to be fitted with ancillary machinery of all descriptions; galleys (kitchens) and storerooms installed; bracketry fitted to take beautifully carved and polished panelling for which the ship would become famous; in passenger areas bare steel pillars that supported one deck from another were prepared to be encased with crafted mahogany columns and beautiful, cast capitals; fittings such as anchors and cables installed; electrical generators securely fitted with tentacles of carefully concealed cabling extending all over the ship; and a thousand other tasks both great and small. Work areas were painted; toilets and bathrooms tiled in lino or ceramic; passenger areas were laid with lino or carpeted; and upper decks were prepared to take deck planking, each seam waterproofed with caulking.

Each piece of machinery, equipment, seasoned timber, etc. had to be manufactured and taken to the ship, and the fittings that the shipyard could not manufacture were sub-contracted to firms all over the country and delivered by rail. The main massive castings, products of the heavy engineering that dominated British industry at the time, were ordered from a trio of foundries. Stem and stern posts that had been erected during the building of the ship had been supplied by the Darlington Forge Company, while anchor cables that weighed 132 tons and were 1,900ft long (at the time the largest anchor chains ever made), and mooring chains used to moor against a specially built buoy, The Cunard, on the River Mersey, were built by Brown Lenox & Co. Ltd at their Newbridge chainworks in Pontypridd, Mid Glamorgan. The two main 10-ton anchors and the kedging anchor stowed on the fo'c'sle came from Messrs N. Hingley & Sons, Ltd, of Netherton near Dudley in the West Midlands. Samples of the Welsh-made chain links were tested well above their specification by Lloyd's Register, who found them practically indestructible.

After the last of the boilers, their fronts made by the Leeds Forge Company, were shipped the hatchways in the upper deck were closed and the erection of the funnels began. Gradually over the following days these were completed, rising 153ft above the baseline of the ship. Lifeboat davits were installed, teak decks laid and a myriad of other essential works undertaken.

Meanwhile, while the bustle continued on the outside of the ship and in the engine and boiler rooms, other trades – Joiners, Carpenters, Painters, Polishers, Fitters, etc. from sub-contracted firms – erected the magnificent panelling that would become the trademark of the ship. Using designs by Harold Peto, the carved and gilded woodwork had been fashioned by joinery firms in London and Newcastle, disassembled and taken to the ship for re-erection, covering primed steel bulkheads that carried scrawled names of many of the men who had worked so far on the liner. These names would lay hidden for many, many years until the ship's final moments revealed them once again.

With her launch coat of grey still pristine, the *Mauretania* takes on a heavy load from the floating crane, *Titan*. The tip of the liner's forward starboard propeller, also with its launch paint, can be seen with men working alongside it. This tip would sink lower into the water as the ship increased in weight as she took on more of her fittings.

The ship's cylindrical, double-ended boilers were of the Morison suspension type, 22ft long and about 17ft 3in in diameter, each end having four furnaces, and were placed in four boiler rooms. Two single-ended boilers (12ft long) were seated along with five double-ended in the foremost boiler room, No. 5. The last of the twenty-three boilers is seen here being placed on board by the floating crane, *Titan*. The installation would feed the turbines with steam at a pressure of up to 195psi and the ship, along with her sister, exceeded any 'installation previously fitted on board ship' by 75 per cent. Together the 192 furnaces would consume much of the 6,000 tons of coal taken on for each crossing of the North Atlantic.

An essential aid in British heavy engineering was the steam hammer that shaped many great forgings. In not-so-far-away Hanley, Stoke-on-Trent, one young school leaver operated such a hammer at the Etruria Forge until his love of the sea took him away, and he eventually reached high command. His name was E.J. Smith and he achieved undying fame when he took command of his final ship – *Titanic*.

The sturdy foundry men of Pontypridd (the men probably belonging to the magnificently named Chainmakers' and Strikers' Association) stand by one of their amazing creations – the ship's incredibly strong anchor chains. Each 170lb link, forged from 3¾in-diameter steel bars, was 22½in long and 13½in wide. The cross-brace (stay pin) was a device conjured up by the foundry's co-founder, Samuel Brown.

JOHN BELLAMY, L^{D.}

GENERAL
ENGINEERS,
TANK
AND
BOILERMAKERS.

CONTRACTORS
TO
ADMIRALTY
AND
WAR OFFICE.

MILLWALL,   LONDON.

MOORING BUOY SPECIALLY CONSTRUCTED FOR CUNARD O.T.S.S. "LUSITANIA."

Another product of Wales were massive mooring shackles that would be attached to the huge buoy – The Cunard Buoy, manufactured at Millwall on the Thames – that would be set in the River Mersey. This huge buoy would be used when the ships were coaling or waiting to berth alongside the Princes Landing Stage to take on passengers.

The 'front men' of any ship were mighty castings – the anchors – on which could depend the safety of a ship, its cargo and passengers. Those for the *Mauretania* were of the 'Hall's patent improved type' and were cast at Messrs N. Hingley & Sons foundry at Netherton. The anchor shown weighed 10 tons, the largest then made until the advent of the *Olympic* four years later at 15½ tons (then exceeded by ¼ ton by her sister, *Titanic*).

With three-and-a-half funnels in place, a large fitting is lowered into the rapidly completing ship.

Deckhouses are built and (except for the after house) painted, lifeboats are stowed, a few shell side doors and coal ports open, but the on-board temporary boilers that provided on-board power are still in place as smoke issues from the one placed forward. All four funnels have been erected.

Although still without the highlighting paintwork on her relief draught marks, but with all lifeboats secure and coal ports open in readiness to receive a set amount of coal for her Builder's Trials, an almost complete liner signals her eagerness to be off by sounding her whistle, perhaps for the first time.

Clockwise from above: Although shown with its soon-to-be-fitted greenery, the open Verandah Cafe on the Boat Deck and sited aft of the Smoking Room already looks inviting and ready to welcome its first passengers to enjoy a cup of coffee.

The superb fireplace, described as one of many 'notable achievements of British craftsmanship', was sited in the 11ft-high First-Class Smoking Room. Carved out of solid walnut, its frieze was modelled on a work by Della Robbia, and the sides of the fireplace were lined with marble.

The vaulted First-Class Smoking Room looking forward measured 52ft long and 50ft wide, and was decorated in fifteenth-century Italian style. This comfortable room, along with many others, was superbly designed by famed architect and garden designer Harold Peto. The woodwork was built by three firms: W. Turner Lord & Co. of London; Robson & Sons of Newcastle; and Mellier & Co., also of London. Other woodwork and joinery was completed by the yard's own Joiners Shop under the company's Head Joiner, W.C. Phipps.

The drawing room of one of two Regal Suites sited one on each side of the Promenade Deck. The Adams-style portside drawing and dining rooms were panelled in East India satinwood, skilfully veneered so that the veneers converged in the middle of each panel; gilding abounded, and the wallpaper was of green silk. The starboard side equivalent was panelled in fiddle-back sycamore with wall coverings in rose and carpeting in a similar colour.

The dining room of a Regal Suite seen from the adjoining drawing room. There were two bedrooms (one single, the other twin) in a Georgian style finished in white with mahogany furniture as well as a bathroom with a tub and a separate WC.

The Library and Writing Room was a beautiful space with its panelling of sycamore 'stained a silver grey' with gilding having a matching slightly greenish tinge. The rose-coloured carpets, curtains and upholstery showed off the detail in the crystal chandeliers, overhead dome and the bevelled glazing of the bookshelves. The roundel carving of the slender supporting panels between the bookcases saw a simplified resurrection in the decor of the corridors leading to the Main Dining Room on the later *Queen Mary 2* almost a century later.

Opposite: With the Library and Writing Room forward and the Lounge and Music Room with its marvellous tapestries aft, the Grand Entrance of the Boat Deck boasted a novel installation: a double lift (elevators) that descended six decks to the Lower Deck, with staircases on either side. Fine, rare woods were sourced from both England and France for the panelling and columns; India rubber tiles were laid on the well-used deck; green carpets graced the stairs; but the elevator grilles that emulated fifteenth-century ironwork were made of a (then) unusual metal – aluminium – which gave a great saving in weight.

... and two to six people in the upper dining room on chairs upholstered in deep pink.

The Dining Saloons were, in fact, one tall room 28ft high split into two by a balcony, all overlooked by an outstanding cream and gold groined dome, with its tracery junctions marked by circular panels elegantly depicting the signs of the zodiac. Panelling was of straw-coloured oak, much of which had been skilfully carved into high relief with no allowance for repetition. The long communal tables that were the norm in First Class at one time were replaced by tables that could seat five to fourteen in the lower ...

Both Second and Third Class still retained the old-style long trestle tables in their respective dining rooms. Third Class is illustrated with its basic panelling, enamelled deck-head and swivel chairs. Second Class was finished rather more grandly with carved panelling and a covered deck-head/ceiling and more ornately finished chairs.

Food preparation was undertaken in galleys, with First and Second Classes sharing the same kitchen sited between the two dining rooms on the Upper Deck ('C').

The First-Class Pantry. The pantries for Second and Third Class were about a quarter of the size of this!

Opposite: With many of her coal ports open, the *Mauretania* appears to be readying for her Preliminary (Builder's) Trials, during which her builders will put her engines etc. to the test. A specified amount of coal would be shipped so that the liner would start her trials at a specified draught. Draughts would be taken before each trial as the ship rose in the water and this would indicate how much coal had been burned.

Always a point of special interest to those travelling across the Tyne by ferry, the *Mauretania* was also a sightseer's joy and many would view the great Cunarder from small steamers such as the *Tynesider*. (Collection of Eric K. Longo)

Clockwise from left: The eyes of the liner with bell, binnacle, telegraphs and transmitters installed on a spacious Bridge. The domain of the Captain and his navigating officers, theirs was a world of ringing, polished, gleaming brass instruments largely supplied by renowned manufacturer Chadburn's.

A sign that the liner was ready to embark on her Builder's Trials, the lifeboats are safely stowed in their davits. Lifeboat regulations, as stipulated by the Board of Trade in 1896, were that ships over 10,000 tons needed only to carry sixteen boats. The *Mauretania* exceeded this by 350 per cent! Increases in ships' sizes were not reflected by an increase in boat numbers. Passenger numbers did not come into the Board's equation.

Viewed on a misty day in the shipyard, a still-untidy After or Poop Deck (with massive hemp and sisal mooring ropes waiting to be coiled neatly) clearly demonstrates the construction of a large ship. The Poop Deck itself is part of the Shelter Deck or, more technically, the Strength Deck – the uppermost deck of the 'ship girder' on which, in the days of sail, single-height deckhouses would have been built. Over the years further deckhouses were built atop the single house with deck-heads extending outwards to provide promenade space. Just aft of one of two large capstans (foreground) can be seen the warping winch and to the right (inboard of the notice board mounted outboard of the railings) would have been a strengthened deck-mount (concealed) on which one of twelve 6in cannon could be mounted in time of war, thus converting the liner into the fast AMC for which she had been built. This working area of the liner doubled as a minimal and oft-crowded promenade space for Third-Class passengers. Behind the bulkhead of the deckhouse built immediately on to the Shelter Deck are the Second-Class gentlemen's toilets and communal bathrooms, with other Second-Class accommodation forward of that, and the house above showing a double doorway gave entrance to the Second-Class Smoke Room on the Promenade Deck with the Boat Deck above. Both latter decks comprised Second-Class promenades. Towering over all is the After Docking Bridge, from where an eye could be kept on activities on the Poop Deck during mooring manoeuvres (once the Third-Class passengers had been cleared from the deck) and orders relayed via telegraphs. The Bridge sits atop a 'cubby hole' that, it is presumed, was a deck store housing oil lamps, etc..

A superb photograph, taken from the top of the building gantry over Nos 1 and 2 Building Slips, showing the completed *Mauretania* lying alongside the specially built dolphins, and the wide access gangway leading to the ship.

At the receiving end of the bridge telegraphs was the Starting (control) Platform – the nerve centre of the ship – in the Engine Room. An Aladdin's cave of gleaming brass and copper dials, gauges and wheels, this relatively cool place controlled the amount of steam passing into the turbines by turning the large brass wheels seen in the illustration. Steam production was regulated by bells that rang at set intervals by each boiler – the faster the ship was required to go, the more steam was required to be fed into the turbines, which, in turn, meant that the boiler bells sounded with greater frequency. This required faster, increased back-breaking work for the firemen feeding the furnaces and for the trimmers supplying coal from the bunkers.

EPISODE 7

PRELIMINARY (BUILDER'S) TRIALS, 17 SEPTEMBER 1907

September 1907 was a very busy month for the Cunard Steamship Company. On the 7th – and to great acclaim – the mighty *Lusitania* (the first of the New Cunarders) had left Liverpool on her maiden voyage and just missed taking the coveted Blue Riband from the Germans by a paltry thirty minutes after encountering fog. She would, undoubtedly, show her mettle on her next crossing.

Ten days later, on Tuesday, 17 September on Tyneside, another great event was due to take place. The Summer had been notably cold and had seen terrific thunderstorms, and the forecast for this special day predicted west-to-south-westerly moderate-to-fresh winds with the possibility of showers. But this did not dampen the spirited enthusiasm of not only the local populace but of many who travelled specially to Tyneside for the day's celebrations.

After many months of careful fitting out and initial testing of equipment, the *Mauretania*, the 'Wonder of the Age', was ready to embark on her next great adventure, her first journey to the sea, in order to be tested in her natural element by her builders. These Builder's Trials would prove to her makers that they had produced a sound ship and that everything

was in good working order. A second set of trials testing her speed-making abilities would come later.

After spending just three days under a year at her fitting-out berth on the 'Mucky Tyne', her underwater hull had accumulated an amount of marine growth that was expected to affect her performance when at sea. She was also not looking her best, the grey paint of her launch having weathered with streaks of staining running down her sides – she would receive her gorgeous make-up when the trials had been completed. But, in spite of this, she did her best to look as distinguished as possible as befell her status as now the world's largest liner, and her huge white ventilators – with their distinctive semi-spherical cowl tops with red-painted interiors – had been arranged to face smartly forward like a procession of rather portly, red-faced Carthusian monks!

Eleven hundred men had boarded the vessel earlier that morning, including 500 from the builder's technical staff, craftsmen, tradesmen and representatives of Cunard. Among this group the builder's technical men would take readings from all over the ship during the forthcoming four days of trials, collating their results after each day's work from readings of temperatures, revolutions, fuel and water consumptions, draughts, etc. The 'workshop' staff would finish jobs or adjust equipment where needed. To guide her down the stream she had River Pilot Thomas Young on board accompanied by Captain Thomas White, who would pilot the ship during her trials on the North Sea. Cunard's own Captain John Pritchard was also on board as an observer; he had been appointed as the liner's first commander. Once she had been accepted by the company and was in service, any early information her Captain could glean about the ship's behaviour on these trials would be invaluable.

At 9.30 a.m. – an hour before high water at the river's entrance – and attended by several tugs (including two Dutch ocean-going vessels, *Poolzee* and *Oceaan*, the employment of which had been taken as somewhat of a slight by local tug operators), 'The Pride of the Tyne', as she was proudly referred to by Novacastrians, was gently pulled away from her berth, smoke belching from her four lofty funnels as her engines were prepared to get under way. Local tugs *Washington*, *Gauntlet*, *Snowden* and *President* acted as bridesmaids on this auspicious departure.

Huge crowds had already gathered in the shipyard and on both banks of the river downstream towards the sea. Cheering accompanied the ship during her progress; schoolchildren, given a very special holiday for the occasion, would remember this day for the rest of their lives.

The excitement of the moment was also felt by those on board, and those not involved with the navigation and operation of the liner leant over, or stood on, the rails to look down and wave at the mass of craft gathered around the giant vessel. After being gently pulled into mid-stream, the *Mauretania* thrilled under her own steam as telegraph signals from the Bridge rang 'slow ahead' down to the Engine Room. Obeying that command, wheels were turned and her wondrous turbines started the momentum that would move her ahead under her own power, carefully chaperoned by tugs connected by umbilical cables to ensure her safety.

On the river a fleet of pleasure craft had accrued to escort the ship on this, her first journey, and others would join en route – paddle steamers, tugs and private steam launches keeping pace with the ship as she increased her speed to a cautious 4 knots. The Tyne General Ferry Company's *Audrey* was late in leaving her pier and had her work cut out to catch up with the royal progress.

The demanding sea, 7½ miles ahead downstream, beckoned.

With boilers alight and steam sibilating into the gull-startled air, the ship is almost ready to leave the Tyne on Builder's Trials. Her launch-grey hull is streaked from an inactive, weather-beaten year spent alongside her dolphins. (Collection of Charles Haas and Jack Eaton)

At 9.30 a.m., surrounded by smoke and excitement, the *Mauretania*, under the solicitous care of tugs, edges out from her berth. A signal, comprised of a square black flag and a black ball, is hoisted aft on her Main Mast, indicating that vessels other than her tugs should keep at a safe distance as she was being navigated at a low speed with reduced manoeuvrability. Finally, in mid-stream, the *Mauretania*, under her own steam, turned to point downriver and her whistles started to sound in what would be an almost continuous salute to those on shore and afloat who had come to wish her success. (*The Bystander*)

Clockwise from left: After steaming at about 4 knots, the liner passed near to Palmer's shipyard at Jarrow where many of the population on the Durham side of the river, dressed in their Sunday best for this very special occasion, watched as the great ship steamed slowly by. (Collection of Kevin Blair)

Still in The Narrows of the river, she approaches Tynemouth – the estuarine outer harbour at the mouth of the Tyne.

The *Mauretania* passes from The Narrows into Tynemouth with steam vigorously issuing from both sets of whistles. From here she will pick up speed but still under the careful supervision of the *Poolzee* and *Oceaan*. As she passed these points at 10.45 a.m. a great cheer went up from those who watched. A mere mile of river lay between the ship and the open sea!

Before reaching Tynemouth, she passed a training ship, the old 74-gun, ex-third-rate wooden-wall *Wellesley*. On board the boys, rescued from impoverishment ashore and now under training, climbed aloft on the standing rigging from where they sang 'Rule, Britannia!' – their young, eager voices perhaps diminished by boat whistles, cheering and distance. Shortly afterwards, the Lloyd's hailing station and the North Shields fish quay were passed to port where dozens of trawlers and drifters added their raucous greetings.

A superb study of the now-free liner as she yet again salutes those around her in the confines of Tynemouth.

With tow hawsers now slackened, the ship strains for the open sea, as eager as those on board to show of what she is capable.

Surrounding craft increase their speed as they try to keep up with the accelerating liner as she passes into Tynemouth, the high hill of Tynemouth Cliffs topped by the Percy Square barracks. Below the cliffs lay The Flats and, just to the east of them, lay the notorious rocks of the Black Middens, the consumer of many a fine ship:

> Oh! the Cliffs of Old
> Tynemouth they're wild and
> they're sweet,
> And dear are the waters that
> roll at their feet;
> And the old ruined Abbey, it
> ne'er shall depart;
> 'Tis the star of my fancy, the
> home of my heart ...

... until, finally freed from the tugs' hawsers, the magnificent ship gathers speed and forges ahead, smoke and steam flowing aft in an almost horizontal stream. (Ambrose Greenway)

In the Marine Park at South Shields two elderly sages, probably giving their considered judgement on the new wonder, watch the liner as she steams to pass between the two piers that guard the entrance to Tynemouth.

The northern extremity of the trials was the manned lighthouse standing atop St Abb's Head. She is seen steaming here at full speed towards the end of a northerly run in this photograph by John Wood. Despite having a bottom fouled with marine growth after lying in the river for a year, she produced magnificent results. She began her daily half-hourly runs (one trial was a double transit of the course) at 2.10 p.m. to the north on 18 September and achieved the following top mean speeds during the four days of the trials:

Wednesday, 18 September 24.93 knots.
Thursday, 19 September 24.93 knots
Friday, 20 September 25.99 knots (on one run she made 26.27 knots!)
Saturday, 21 September Following some slow speed runs she was run at 23 knots ahead then put full speed astern, achieving this manoeuvre in forty-five seconds. It took three minutes fifty-eight seconds to stop the vessel in about ¾ mile.

Her specification had required 24½ knots at about 60,000hp – her projected results indicated 26 knots at 65,000hp and a projected horsepower of 80,000 to give 27!

Due to Admiralty involvement, many of the results achieved were confidential and not released to the press. As wireless transmissions could be intercepted, an unusual method was adopted to send messages ashore securely – carrier pigeons!

The liner is about to pass through the piers at the mouth of the river. The open sea lies ahead, along with whatever the next few days will bring.

Probably taken by John Wood, the *Mauretania* has turned twenty-five minutes after her run to the north on the measured mile and is seen returning on the southern leg of a trial. The swiftly ploughed sea is curling away from her bow in a graceful arc and the wave re-emerging at her waist amidships. The lighthouse keepers seem to be more interested in the still-novel camera! The results of these trials were generally kept secret due to Admiralty caution.

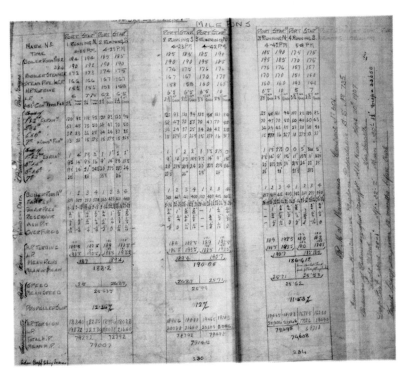

An unpublished sheet from the Preliminary Trials for Friday, 20 September 1907. Even though an average was taken from a double run (with and against the tide), a close study of the pencilled results shows that on her run commencing at 4.23 p.m. she achieved an incredible 26.27 knots! – even more remarkable as the 'vessel [had] been lying in the river for twelve months' without a dry-docking to clean the marine growth accumulated on her bottom plates. At the end of each day's trials the *Mauretania* anchored off the mouth of the Tyne, probably with ports alight for display. One correspondent wrote: 'Spent yesterday at Shields. Saw the *Mauretania* anchor off the North Pier. She lies there every night during her preliminary trials. She is a grand sight.'

With exhaust steam exuding from her safety valves, this photograph may have been taken as she returned – almost breathless in her excitement – to the Tyne after the completion of her trials. She would make another triumphant arrival into the river, conveniently timed for a Saturday afternoon after the morning's trials, when workers had finished their morning shifts and obviating another special school holiday.

The *Mauretania* steamed inwards between Tynemouth's guardian piers at 12.50 p.m. on 21 September with a Dutch tug taking her forward hawser and locals tugs attending aft. Lining both shores of the river, an estimated 50,000 people excitedly waited to welcome her home from her great successes over the past four days.

As she steamed towards the Fish Dock, the nearby white-painted weatherboard Lloyd's hailing station signalled the traditional challenge: 'What ship?', and reportedly received the reply: '*Mauretania*. What town?'

A few minutes later, at 1 p.m., the *Mauretania* came to a halt between the Albert Edward Dock at Coble Dene with its staithes, twenty steam and hydraulic cranes, timber yards and warehouses to the north, and 'Old Ballast Hill' (there was more than one!) at South Shields on the opposite bank. To watch her arrival and to see her next manoeuvre, a huge crowd and an atmosphere 'like a Holliday [sic] with the Big Ship coming in. You ought to have seen the Crowds' had gathered at, 'Every place [where] a view was to be got'.

By now a second Dutch tug was in attendance and, after the liner had come to a halt, the tugs began to turn her 180 degrees: 'it was a rare sight to see them swinging her in mid-stream.' The operation took twenty-five minutes to complete but, in a heart-stopping moment, the big ship began a worrying drift towards the northern shore, submerging a mooring buoy as she did so.

At 1.30 p.m., after regaining control, the tugs began the tow astern, back to the liner's dolphins at Wallsend, passing Jarrow, Howden and Hebburn as they did so, where the liner was secured, suitably pointing downstream to the open sea to await the next big episode.

FAREWELL TO HOME: THE OFFICIAL TRIALS

Completing her successful Preliminary (Builder's) Trials, the *Mauretania* had returned to the Tyne to moor against her shipyard dolphins facing downstream; a month now separated her from her final departure from the river of her birth, and much work had still to be done, the most obvious to those travelling on the river being the application of tons of paint to present her in the livery of her owners-in-waiting – the Cunard Steamship Company. Not so obvious was the completion of her internal decoration and the addition of internal stiffening aft to assist in obviating vibration experienced during her trials at high speed (probably due to the propeller type).

Gleaming black paint (unbroken except for sparkling brass portholes that surrounded thick glass 'lights' that reflected the river's blackened shimmer) gradually covered her hull up to 'B'-deck and on her upper-works white paint, just as gleaming, prevailed – a colour that persuaded potential passengers that the smart ship was clean and smut-free. Her conspicuous funnels by now, after a year of weathering and faded to almost an orange, were repainted in the bright, pristine carmine red of Cunard, circumscribed with the company's three distinctive black lines, all topped by a broad, soot-disguising capping of black.

Activity abounded inside the ship as Engineers, Fitters, Joiners, Carpet Fitters, Polishers, Cleaners, Painters and a myriad of other tradesmen and contractors busied themselves to complete their tasks. Stores were taken on including hundreds of tons of good Durham coal mined locally from the pits in the south-east of the county – enough to get her to Liverpool, where the best Welsh steam coal (from a dedicated pit that mined coal *only* for the *Lusitania* and *Mauretania*, Royal Yachts and warships on trials) would be taken on for the most important series of her trials, the 'Officials'. Good coal such as this weighed 50–55lb per cubic foot and the ship had bunker space for 6,000 tons, of which 5,000 would be consumed on each Atlantic crossing; a Fireman's shovel-load weighed about 12lb and he fed up to 4 tons of 'King Coal' into his hungry furnaces during a four-hour watch.

On 17 October the completing liner was opened to the public gaze and, in spite of being on a weekday (Thursday), 23,000 tickets had been sold at *2s 6d* (half a crown or 12½p) to expectant and soon-to-be-impressed visitors, the monies raised being given to local charities.

On the morning of 22 October 1907 (a month after her return from her Preliminary Trials), and as the liner lay sedately at her berth, her mentor, the diminutive *Turbinia* – the mother of all turbine steamers – came alongside and snuggled beneath the flare of the liner's overhanging starboard bow. It had been intended that the yacht should precede the great ship in her progress down the Tyne but a mechanical fault precluded this spectacle and the *Mauretania* would eventually proceed downstream alone without her matron of honour. Another special holiday had been declared on Tyneside for the day's celebration, and thousands yet again converged towards vantage points along the river's banks from which to witness this great event.

At 2 p.m. the *Mauretania* was eased away from her dolphins and, in doing so, severed her link with the shores that had built her.

The skilled and emotional fortune that had been expended on this pinnacle of engineering and aesthetic achievement was about to mature into becoming 'The Pride of the Tyne'.

On Thursday, 17 October 1907, 23,000 ticket holders trooped on board to marvel at the wonders of what local industry had produced. Many families of those who had been involved with the building and fitting out of the ship could now see and be impressed by their menfolk's skill. Five days later, on 22 October, forever to remain in the annals of Tyneside as a day to remember – the *Mauretania* was joined by the diminutive *Turbinia*, which, as has been related, nestled beneath the giant liner's bow. (Estate of the late Captain John Pritchard/Author's collection)

As the liner progresses down the 'Mucky Tyne', the specially invited guests are as absorbed by the passing scene as those on shore are by the departing vessel. Here one well-heeled guest balances precariously on the ship's rail while another supports him to help steady the former's camera!

After many years of anticipation – and with Captain John Pritchard on the Bridge – the liner slowly broke her connection with the land as tugs carefully pull her away from her mooring dolphins. The *Ceylan*, being completed for the French steamship line Compagnie Maritime des Chargeurs Reunis, lays over on the port side of the much larger liner's moving bow.

Opposite: The liner's progress downriver was almost a repeat of her departure on her Preliminary Trials but this time it was not anticipated that she would return. As she passed the Fish Dock, the fishing vessels there bade a raucous farewell to their giant sister in what must have sounded like a discordant steam organ, as American poet Vachel Lindsay once said, 'Tooting joy, tooting hope!' Steaming out into the outer harbour of Tynemouth, the liner began to pick up speed as cheering resounded from the shore. Steam, smoke and noise made a heady mix and a correspondent wrote on a postcard: 'Mother. I went to Tynemouth yesterday to see the Mauretania Leave the Tyne. It was well worth seeing. I wish you had been there. There were thousands …' The illustration shows one of a series of evocative photographs taken by local photographer Gladstone Adams of Whitley Bay (18 Station Road) as his boat motors ahead of and crosses the path of the oncoming ship. This picture is taken from a first-generation print issued by the photographer's studio.

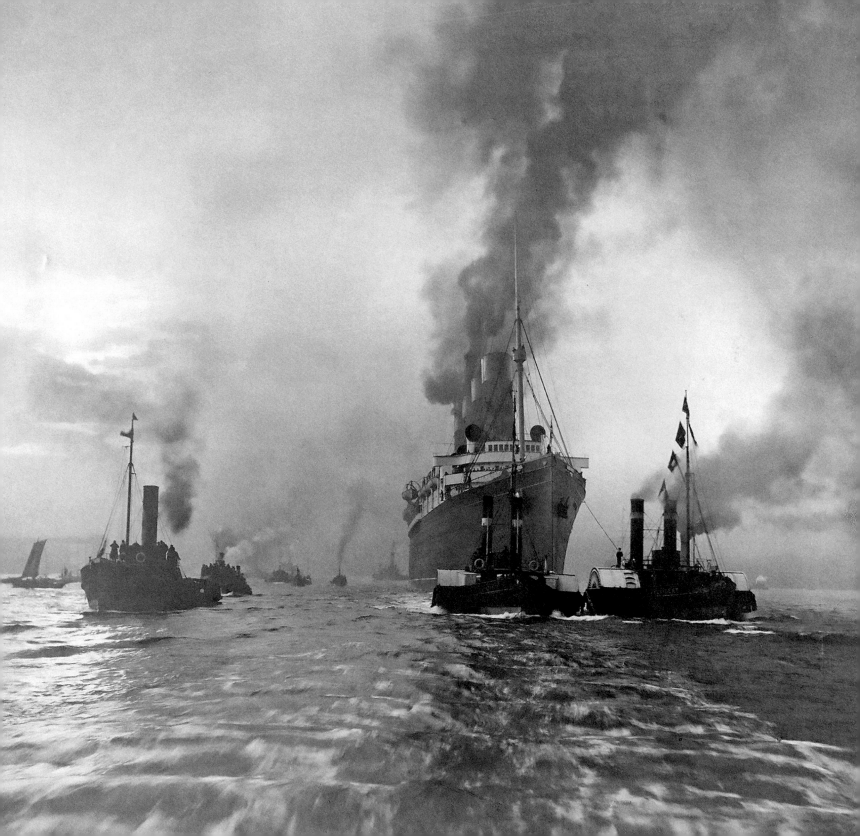

After passing between the North and South Piers that guarded the entrance to Tynemouth, the *Mauretania* came to a brief stop to adjust compasses before starting on her 'North About' navigation around the Scottish coast. Mary, Lady Inverclyde, was on board and, after being presented with a golden bracelet of tiny turbine blades surrounding a rotor, she rang the Bridge telegraph for the ship to go ahead. The press had been told that no data would be taken on this delivery trip but technicians would, in fact, be kept busy taking readings and making notes.

A view of the ship's Boat Deck taken from a brochure illustrates the Boat Deck promenade, somewhat restricted by the lifeboats, for perambulating passengers.

Senior Cunard and technical guests gather for a group photograph. Among several who can be identified are George Hunter (middle front, seated); John Wigham Richardson (front, second from right, seated); Leonard Peskett (Cunard's Naval Architect – back row to left of steam pipe); Captain John Pritchard (standing behind George Hunter); and, standing to the Captain's left, is Lord Brassey, publisher of *Brassey's Naval Annual* that listed and illustrated both *Mauretania* and *Lusitania* as AMCs that could outrun those of a belligerent nation.

Being the second of two ships, the new liner's arrival in Liverpool did not elicit the same excitement as the *Lusitania*'s did a few months earlier. This photograph is undated but could easily represent how the ship appeared on that first arrival.

The *Mauretania* is guided carefully through the entrance to the Sandon Dock ...

... before being moored against the basin wall.

Taken from the pages of *The Shipbuilder*, the *Mauretania* is seen here in the Gladstone dry dock, where the remains of the launching gear was removed and her bottom cleaned of a year's worth of marine growth and painted. After being coaled with a specific amount of the fuel (to get her down to a pre-determined draught, the decrease of which was noted during trials and thus indicating her use of bunkers), she was ready for the all-important Official Trials. If she performed well on these then she would be accepted by Cunard.

Moored mid-stream with trials signals raised, the *Mauretania* is being coaled.

The classic photograph of the *Mauretania*! A superb study of the great liner at speed on the Skelmorlie Measured Mile, with the Cloche Lighthouse on the distant shore. Her paintwork at her entry into the water has been eroded by the speed at which she was travelling. (Ambrose Greenway Collection)

At the time of writing the following photographs posed a problem of identification in both time and sequence – is the *Mauretania* being towed out of dock (stern first) or is she arriving back in Liverpool? It is probably the former as her funnels show no sign of weathering (as in the final photograph), but they do serve to show the tightness of her entry through the dock gates.

Went through "Mauretania", Wednesday, Nov: 27th

Trials – Elegance in Motion. Impressive at full speed, this photograph was used as a postcard to give an impression of the liner's everyday steaming, hence the added American flag of destination flying at her foretruck! She was scheduled to undertake three sets of trials: the first consisted of two double passes of the Irish Sea to St George's Channel (average 26.17 knots) to test her endurance and fuel consumption, which would give an indication of her ability to meet the stipulations of the 1903 agreement. She made two double passes of this course, which represented a half-crossing of the North Atlantic, without pause. Progressive speed trials were then undertaken on the Skelmorlie Measured Mile, during which her speed was, of course, progressively increased on the various runs (average 26.54 knots). Finally, there were speed tests over a greater set distance, Ailsa Craig to Holy Island off Scotland's Isle of Arran (average 26.75 knots). (Collection of Eric K. Longo)

Again a speculative assumption that this shows the liner at the end of her successful trials. One black signal has already been lowered and her fourth funnel shows signs of staining. The tall chimney belches smoke from the boiler of the pumping engine that empties the dry dock, while White Star liners sit at their berths beyond.

FROM MAIDEN TO QUEEN OF THE OCEAN (1907–29)

The early evening of Saturday, 16 November 1907, was cold and wet. Some 200,000 people had turned out to see the *Lusitania* depart on her maiden voyage three months earlier on a more clement and balmier 7 September, but now the rain deterred a similar send-off for her slightly larger sister with just a quarter of that number, armed with glistening umbrellas, braving the weather to wish her 'bon voyage'.

As with her sister, the *Mauretania* carried the hopes of a nation that she would confirm the former's victory over the German competition and help to consolidate for Great Britain the recently regained and much coveted Blue Ribband. The government (through the Admiralty) knew that she could outrun and catch any enemy merchant ship in her guise as an AMC, and the Post Office knew that, as a Royal Mail Ship (the 'RMS' of her title), she would transport valuable business mails – as well as Granny's Christmas cards – expeditiously across the North Atlantic between the powerful nations on either side of 'the Pond'. Severe penalties awaited imposition by the Postmaster General if she did not.

Crew had been signed on and Third-Class passengers joined the ship while she was moored against the Cunard Buoy in the River Mersey, being tendered aboard from 12 noon. Just after 3 p.m., the liner moved to her departure berth alongside the Princes Landing Stage, from where the other two classes of passenger would board.

At 7.36 p.m. the spectators were rewarded with the sight of the *Mauretania* pulling away from the Stage, her next stop Queenstown (Cobh), where she would anchor while mails and passengers were tendered out to her. The call into the southern Irish port would prove to be contentious as, not only would the ship have to pause just as she was getting into her pace, but should the mails from London via Dublin be delayed for any reason then the mighty ship would be delayed herself. In spite of Cunard's entreaties, the Postmaster General kept the company to its agreement.

As any journey has a beginning and (hopefully) an end, and as depictions of speed can be elusive, the following illustrations are included to show the landfalls between which the *Mauretania* made her voyages – of which some were record-breaking – that changed over the years. In 1908 the Welsh port of Fishguard was introduced (as will be seen later) as a homeward port of call and, after 1919, when Cunard's express service transferred to Southampton, Plymouth eventually became the first landfall for the early delivery of mails and some of her British-bound passengers before the liner sailed to Cherbourg to discharge her continental passengers. Southampton had now become her terminus – her new home port. Over the years, the durations of crossings varied (depending on season and ports of call) but her average speed for each crossing was taken from distances steamed from noon to noon.

As related, the morning of the *Mauretania*'s maiden voyage from the great seaport of Liverpool had been spent at the Cunard Buoy on the Sloyne, where the crew had been mustered prior to fire and boat drills being carried out. From noon Third-Class passengers were tendered out to her and, three or four hours later, she transferred alongside the Princes Landing Stage, where those travelling in Saloon (First) and Second Class would board without having to cope with mixing with those in Third.

In command of the great liner was Captain John Pritchard. A native of Caernarfon in Wales, the experienced Captain was 61 years of age and started his sea-going career at the age of 13 as a ship's cook on a sailing schooner carrying coal. He rose through the ranks until gaining his Master's Certificate at the age of 29. He joined the Cunard Steamship Company in 1880. (Courtesy of Eric K. Longo)

The *Mauretania*'s first stay in New York was not without incident as within the vicinity of the ship a gang of about 100 revolver-wielding Italian coal-passers rioted, which involved revolvers – fortunately there were no fatalities. Three days later, at 12.15 p.m. on a fine but breezy Saturday, 30 November, and with great enthusiasm from hundreds of well-wishers on shore, the liner backed out into the Hudson River (aka the North River) from Pier 54 and headed downstream, passing as she did so the famed Battery Park in lower Manhattan (with the famous clock and two chimneys of the Colgate factory distinguished on the eastern, opposite shore) towards the Statue of Liberty in the Lower Bay and onwards towards the open sea. She passed Sandy Hook at 2.21 p.m., thus beginning her first eastward crossing of the North Atlantic. Among those on board was Albertha Spencer-Churchill, Duchess of Marlborough, and all were eagerly awaiting the ship to take the record for the crossing. Much to the delight and excitement of the ship's crew, her passengers and England as a nation, that ambition was achieved when the liner beat her Scots-built sister's record by 0.08 of a knot, the *Lusitania* having beaten her German rivals by a similar small margin with 23.61 knots that October. Although it would take another two years for the *Lusitania* to relinquish the westward record, the *Mauretania* would then hold both until 1929. A truly remarkable achievement.

A typical photograph of the *Mauretania* in her home river, the Mersey.

Through the night the liner steamed southwards at 20 knots and by morning the weather had much improved with the promise of a brighter day. Just before 8.30 p.m., the Irish pilot boarded and soon the Cunarder was anchored off Roche's Point as she awaited passengers and the all-important mails to be tendered out from Queenstown (Cobh). At 10.45, and with very little wind, the liner set sail for New York. However, the ship experienced only a few hours of peaceful sailing. Unfortunately the fine weather did not last as, eight hours into the North Atlantic, the vessel met a gale that became so severe that she was pitching 60ft into the onslaught – she would become famous for her roll! By 3 p.m. on Monday the spare anchor on the foc's'le broke loose from its fastenings and, with its massive chain, started a rampage about the deck. Captain Pritchard had the ship turned about to steam at 4 knots and personally led a party to secure the recalcitrant equipment. Newspapers published artists' renditions of this heroic but dangerous event and depicted the Captain as a tall, bearded, almost youthful mariner, when in fact Captain Pritchard, an experienced mariner from Wales and near to retirement, was – dare it be said – thickening about the waist. (Collection of Senan Moloney)

The newly arrived but battered liner attracted a large crowd of spectators. Here a gentleman poses at the end of the dock with the ship berthed, still shrouded in the lingering mist, at the still-incomplete Pier 54 at West 13th Street. (Collection of Eric K. Longo)

WHERE THE MAURETANIA TORE THE IRON BITTS FROM PIER

THE LIGHTER CRUSHED AND SUNK BY THE MAURETANIA

The second voyage was nearly as adventuresome as the first. Before the westward crossing had even begun the liner was caught by a strong wind on the Mersey and dragged her anchor, grounding on a hard shingle shelf on the Egremont side of the river. She was safely towed off without leakage (if there had been she would have been urgently dry-docked). However, she would later have several buckled bottom plates replaced.

As the liner made the crossing, she rammed her way at speed through the heavy wintry seas, still without the opportunity of proving her full potential to an eagerly waiting public. Arrival in New York on 21 December 1907 did not guarantee a respite as gales assailed her at her berth and the approaching Christmas brought her an early but cruel present when, two days later, a strong gust buffeted her tall side. Her forward mooring ropes strained with such force that three bollards (bits) were pulled out of their quayside foundations with cannon-like reports. The liner drifted helplessly across the dock to the opposite pier and, in doing so, crushed and sank a coal barge that had been discharging its dusty cargo into the ship's bunkers. The barge's skipper only just managed to jump to safety!

The *Mauretania* headed downstream past the famed Battery Park in lower Manhattan. The famous clock and two chimneys of the Colgate factory can be seen on the eastern, opposite shore.

After an oceanic tussle between the *Lusitania* and *Kaiser Wilhelm II*, the *Mauretania* eventually took her sister's record for the Atlantic eastward journey during her last crossing of 1907 with an average speed of 23.69 knots. She would improve on her own record over the following two years until she made an impressive record crossing at 25.88 knots in June 1909. The *Mauretania* then took the westward record (*Lusitania* had held it for two years) with an oft-celebrated crossing between 26 and 30 September with a speed of 26.06 knots in four days, ten hours and fifty-one minutes. In October 1907 the *Mauretania*'s slightly older sister had taken the accolade of the fastest westward crossing of the North Atlantic, at last taking the Blue Ribband from the current German holder, *Deutschland*, which had held the record since 1903 with a speed of 23.15 knots. The *Lusitania* achieved 23.99 knots and would better this in 1908 with increasing records of 24.83 (May 1908); 25.01 (July); and 25.65 knots (August). The competition between the Scottish-built liner and her English-built sister was beginning to get interesting. Other than newer ships with stunning modern decor, there would not be much post-war competition and the *Mauretania* would keep the Ribband for an astounding twenty years. Immensely proud of his ship, Captain Pritchard proudly poses by Lifeboat No. 2 (port side, forward) at the end of his career at sea. New York, 28 December 1909. (Estate of Captain John Pritchard/Author's collection)

After the Great War, the Cunard Express service was transferred to Southampton as it was nearer to both London and the Continent. She is seen in dock to re-store and refuel (a much easier job after the ship was converted to burn oil in 1921) and lays astern of another Cunarder, the *Altonia*, with the United States liner *Leviathan* and, astern of her, the White Star liner *Olympic* in the opposite berths. (Collection of John Skopije)

After a conversion to oil that came about as an indirect result of an on-board fire and a thorough overhaul of her turbines (as will be seen later), the *Mauretania* exceeded her own record when, on the crossing of 20–25 August 1924, she clocked 26.25 knots! Cherbourg had by now been introduced into the ship's itinerary in order to service continental traffic. Here, with the White Star tender *Traffic* alongside, the tender's much larger fleet-mate, *Olympic*, is berthed beyond the distant breakwater. (Unseen, the four-funnelled French liner *France* is astern of *Olympic*.)

As soon as the liner had berthed in Southampton after this record crossing, Cunard manager Mr Cotterell boarded the ship to congratulate Captain Rostron on his ship's fine performance.

Above: Picking up speed as she heads down the Eastern Solent, the fabled Cunarder sails between the forts known as Palmerston's Follies at Spithead.

Left: Dressed overall, the *Mauretania* sits in New York Harbor on a gala occasion. Judging from the worn paint at her entry, this could have been on her arrival in the harbour on 6 August 1929 after attempting to regain her lost record from the German liner *Bremen*. During this westward passage, the Cunarder met with delaying gales and fog (on one day bettering her previous best daily run of 27.04 knots in 1911 by nearly 0.2 knots!) which put her only four hours behind the new champion's time. She was probably too worn to try again.

Opposite: After holding the transatlantic record for a remarkable length of time it was finally taken from her by the German liner *Bremen*, which reached Europe on 22 July 1929 with an average speed of 27.83 knots! A few days later, in August, the liner set out from New York and, ostensibly only known to Captain McNeil and his Chief Engineer, Mr Cockburn, was out to make a fast passage. Indeed, she covered the 3,162 miles between New York and Cherbourg in four days, twenty-one hours and forty-four minutes at a commendable average speed of 26.85 knots. Although this stupendous effort was not quite sufficient to regain the Ribband, she still managed to beat her own record and even achieved a magnificent 29 knots between Plymouth and Cherbourg! Inward-bound at the end of the crossing, she passed another potential record-breaker at the Calshot Spit air station, where a new 'mystery' aircraft, the Gloster-Napier IV (Tail No. 249), was being taken down to the water after undergoing engine trials. This aircraft was Britain's 'new wonder machine' built to compete in the prestigious Schneider Trophy race. Photograph taken on 24 August 1929. (Collection of Derek Olsen)

Back in Southampton after that record run, Chief Engineer Cockburn and Captain McNeil dress in their best on 24 August 1929.

An impressive display of power as the record-breaking *Bremen* is tendered by the diminutive and elderly *Lord Elgin* in The Solent. (Collection of Colin M. Baxter)

EPISODE 10

FISHGUARD

In the early part of the twentieth century advances in technology over the previous several decades had created a demand for speed. A few days saved here ... a few hours there ... meant that the providers of this expensive luxury would be ahead of the competition.

The Cunard Steamship Company was no exception in this field and any improvement in speed – however seemingly small – that would attract the cream of the travellers on the North Atlantic would place their line in an advantageous position. Holding the Blue Riband of the North Atlantic was the best advertisement that ensured that the impressionable and fashionable travelling public was aware of the fastest ship of the day. Emigration, too, was extremely big business with the shipping companies, and the port of Liverpool was well suited for those going westwards from Scandinavia and eastwards from Ireland, but inconvenient for passengers from Europe. In the early twentieth century the company became eager to take advantage of continental traffic, and aspired to follow the lead of their great rival, the White Star Line, which in 1907 moved its express service from Liverpool to Southampton as it was nearer to both London and the Continent. Every Wednesday the line's vessels sailed to the French port of Cherbourg to pick up continental passengers and cargo and then sail on to Queenstown before proceeding to New York. On eastbound crossings White Star called into Plymouth rather than Queenstown to enable London-bound passengers to disembark (thereby saving a few hours on their journey), then proceeded to Cherbourg before terminating the crossing at Southampton. The Hampshire port had other advantages to offer: a double high tide created by the beautiful 'breakwater' of the Isle of Wight, and Southampton Water, which did not have the restriction of a sandbar as did the River Mersey. But for Cunard that was in the future as it was not until after the Great War that the company made the big move south in 1919 when it transferred its express service to the southern port.

The outward call into Queenstown had soon found disfavour with Cunard as it considerably delayed their two new, big express liners, the *Mauretania* and *Lusitania*, by stopping their momentum in order to take on additional mails, as per the 1903 contract with the Postmaster General. Eastward crossings also came under scrutiny and any reductions in the time of travel on the homeward journey that could shorten the journey for passengers who had to get to London, or perhaps Paris, especially for those with important commercial or governmental business, would be an advantage, as White Star had so amply demonstrated to their benefit.

It was with this in mind that the company decided on using Fishguard as an inward port of call en route to Liverpool. Situated on the north-west coast of Pembrokeshire in Wales,

Cunard extolled the placement of Fishguard as being the 'nearest port in Great Britain to New York' and by calling there would reduce the time for passengers to get to London. From the latter half of 1908 both the *Lusitania* and *Mauretania* (as well as other major Cunard ships – *Caronia*, *Carmania*, *Franconia* etc.) started calling in at the developing Welsh port as part of Cunard's 'New Fast Express Route', where a fast train, the famed Great Western Railway's 'Cunard Ocean Express', would whisk the passengers off to London's Paddington Station, the 260-mile journey taking a mere four and three-quarter hours. At one time these express trains would be non-stop but, after a fatal derailment at Salisbury just over two years previously – when an ocean liner express train had taken a 30mph bend at 70 – a brief stop at the cathedral city had become mandatory. A second train would take passengers directly to Dover for the cross-Channel ferries; again, it was hoped, saving precious hours.

The *Mauretania*'s first arrival at Fishguard was on Monday, 30 August 1909 and was the cause of much celebration.

The Great Western Railway had high hopes that Fishguard harbour would become a major port and attract the cream of the North Atlantic trade. To witness the arrival of the world's greatest and fastest liner, thousands of spectators arrived by train, bus, cart, bicycle and by 'Shanks's pony' to line the harbour's edge and the hills overlooking the bay. The morning of the *Mauretania*'s maiden arrival in Fishguard was a gala event. Bunting flew along the harbour front and along the mole – still under construction – and ships in the harbour were gaily decorated with brightly coloured signal flags.

From the early hours a great crowd began to gather and a brass band led a celebratory procession towards the harbour. In this illustration crowds had made a climb to see the ship, along with a cameraman who captured the grand event on to glass-plate negatives. The appearance of the *Mauretania* from around the southern headland of Strumble Head was accompanied by cannon and the explosion of fireworks as steam issued from her funnel vents as she seemed to catch her breath.

With excited observers dressed in their Sunday best looking down at the bay, the *Mauretania*, her wake by now diminishing after a commendably fast crossing at 25.41 knots, glides to her an-chorage. Here waits a vessel that will take her mail and one of two tenders that will disembark passengers who wish to complete a fast voyage: from New York to London in an exciting and unheard of five days – a unique feature that Cunard used to its advantage over its White Star rival!

With a profligacy of bunting lining the edge of the breakwater to mark the momentous occasion, the *Mauretania* glides serenely towards her anchorage.

Bunting now raised and stiffly fluttering from both masts, the now-stilled liner is circled by the craft waiting to attend to her needs.

Passengers on board the famed liner wave for the GWR cameraman on the *Sir Francis Drake*. A series of his photographs would be published as postcards and larger sepia prints.

With flags snapping out brightly to the west'ard, passengers line the liner's decks to watch as (probably) Second-Class passengers descend the gangway leading down to the second tender, the *Smeaton* of 1883, as the discharged baggage slides down another. Many craft sailed around the anchored ship, including the local rowed RNLI lifeboat.

On a carefully cordoned off deck of the General Post Office's steamer, postal workers and smartly uniformed officials wait for the chutes to be erected from the *Mauretania*, down which over 3,000 sacks of mail will cascade before being taken ashore and speedily taken to Southampton by rail for final sorting, arriving there several hours before the ship.

The valuable sacks of mail are quickly placed into large wicker baskets but, as a postal worker clambers over the bundles piled on deck, it seems that some addressees might receive their letters somewhat creased!

The smart new tender *Sir Francis Drake* lay alongside the towering side of the Cunarder to disembark passengers (probably First Class on this tender) and luggage, much of which was affixed with purple labels printed with 'London, via Fishguard' that told all and sundry that the baggage's owner had just travelled in the most modern fashion. Note the exceptionally tall funnels fitted to the *Sir Francis Drake*. It was said that she and her sister, the *Sir Walter Raleigh*, were designed with this feature to lift smoke away from the passengers on the liners.

Well-heeled passengers cross the gangway down to the tender, where ladies might avail themselves of the panelled Ladies' Saloon below decks to avoid the dishevelling breeze during the short passage shore-wards. A General Saloon and a Smoking Room (forward) for gentlemen were also available.

A panoramic view of Fishguard Harbour showing the *Mauretania* beyond the breakwater, where she swung at anchor. The newly developed station sits resplendent in the foreground awaiting the disembarked passengers and mail. The delightful Fishguard Bay Hotel is out of sight snuggled against the side of the hill to the left, past which many sightseers had walked.

Among those who paraded through Fishguard were a group of young ladies in their traditional costume of shawls, chequered or plain-coloured dresses and pinafores, and *hetiau Cymreig* (tall, black hats). The ladies gathered on the quayside to greet each landing passenger with a bunch of Welsh heather.

The passengers landed after the crossing of a lifetime and were quickly ushered to the express trains ...

... that steamingly and impressively awaited at the station. Painted in GWR's green livery with a copper-capped black chimney and, further back, a gleaming brass safety valve cover, two locomotives were being used in tandem (required for heavier trains or for special services such as this one for the *Mauretania*), the lead locomotive being No. 3402 *Halifax*, an Atbara-class 4-4-0. Behind the engines trailed a very comfortable train including Pullman coaches and an immaculate restaurant car, all painted in the famed livery of the Great Western Railway of chocolate brown with cream upper-works. The cosseted passengers would be, as advertised, in London five breathtaking days after leaving New York!

EPISODE 11

DAMAGE, DISASTER AND 'DAMN THE TORPEDOES!'*

For a ship to go through her life without any mishaps would be a rare occurrence – and the *Mauretania* would be no exception.

Her first Captain, John Pritchard, came to the ship well qualified in the experience of drama at sea, having on three occasions while in the employ of the Cunard Steamship Company gone to the rescue of vessels in distress. The most recent was while in command of the then-new *Saxonia*, from which he had led the rescue of two men from an American pilot boat in 1900. Even during the *Mauretania*'s maiden voyage, the Captain had led his men in harnessing a recalcitrant 10-ton spare anchor from creating havoc on the foredeck after shedding its fastenings during a baptismal storm.

To keep a big, fast express ship on schedule meant high speeds even during the worst of North Atlantic weather in all seasons and this involved the *Mauretania* becoming almost literally a 25-knot battering ram pitched in battle against the elements. These assaults on her structure and the constantly changing strains on her well-built hull – her naval architects and shipwrights had done their work well – were immense, so it was unsurprising that her steel plates would suffer the consequences. An early instance was when, before sailing on

her second voyage, she had been blown without power to save herself on to the hard shingle bank off Egremont on the Mersey's Wirral Peninsula, buckling quite a number of bottom plates but fortunately without puncturing her hull in the process.

Ships smaller than the *Mauretania* were less fortunate over the years in the battle against that constant old foe, the weather, and it sometimes befell the great ship to succour those whose lives might otherwise have been lost had she not been there with her speed to effect a rescue.

In 1929 the *Mauretania* surrendered the Blue Riband that she had held for an incredible twenty-two years to the German liner *Bremen*. It was also the year of the Wall Street Crash and the beginning of the Great Depression. The old ship marked the end of the year by colliding with a railway car float, during which three freight cars went overboard.

Other obstacles assailed the ship – either directly or indirectly – whether it was contact with dock walls; encounters with partially submerged derelicts at sea; near collisions with other ships; groundings; shipwreck; or even submarines during wartime. The following pages illustrate some of the peacetime occurrences through which the liner emerged victorious (a later chapter will illustrate her wartime adventures).

* Admiral David Farragut USN

Barely a month had passed before the Cunarder's services were again called upon when she went to the assistance of another coal barge, the *Fall River*, which had broken her tow in a blizzard 80 miles from Sandy Hook. The eastbound liner saw the distress signal just before the vessel sank and fortunately located the small boat, into which the barge's skipper, engineer and deckhand had clambered. Captain Pritchard is seen here in a retirement portrait. (Estate of Captain John Pritchard/ Author's collection)

After a rough second westward crossing, the *Mauretania* arrived in New York on 21 December and is shown here the following day (note the number of mooring ropes and a coaling barge alongside). For the dramatic events of the following day, look at page 93. (Collection of Eric K. Longo)

Captain Pritchard manoeuvred the huge ship to provide a lee to enable the rescue of the men, an act for which he would later be presented with a pair of binoculars on behalf of the President of the United States and a scroll of appreciation as a token of his achievement. (Estate of Captain John Pritchard/Author's collection)

Old Lady (seeing a friend off). "Now, do be careful, dear, and don't forget to give the Captain a shilling to keep off the rocks."

Sage advice about travel insurance!

The *Mauretania* kept to her schedules even during ferocious Atlantic storms, on one occasion arriving a mere eight hours short of her record crossing. Lost propeller blades were a fairly common experience among liners (bronze blades at that time were bolted on to steel bosses) and the *Mauretania* was no exception. Suffering such a loss late in 1908, she also suffered a bent stem (seen here in the process of being removed before being renewed). Cunard stated that she had hit a dock wall but she had probably rammed a derelict as much other damage had been incurred consisting mainly of dented side plates, a lost propeller blade and a seriously fractured bracket that supported the port-side high-pressure turbine shaft. The new propeller shaft wing ('A' bracket) was delivered on a cart pulled by a Wallis and Steevens steam traction engine. The ship spent ten weeks in dry dock from 26 October 1908 and remaining there until 4 January.

During her call into Queenstown at the start of another westward crossing, a Fireman was signed on to the ship's Crew Agreement (he signed with an 'X'). His name was John Coffey (Discharge Book No. 13665) and he gave his last ship as being the *Olympic*, which was duly recorded, but later amended when, a few days later, he came out with the truth. His last ship had not, in fact, been *Olympic* but her sister ship, the *Titanic*, which he had deserted (a punishable offence) a few days earlier. After the disaster that befell the newest of the White Star liners on her maiden voyage, passenger ships hastened to increase their legislated – although woefully inadequate – lifeboat capacities, and this illustration shows *Mauretania* with additional standard boats plus rafts stowed beneath.

The ship's prime role as an ocean liner transporting passengers in comfort across the wide expanse of the North Atlantic was halted in August 1914 when the Great War began to cut its bloody swathe across the course of history. The *Mauretania*'s fine war record will be related in a later episode but two occurrences during the war could have seen her demise and both happened in the Mediterranean Sea. The first occurred at about 6 p.m. on 17 July 1915 when, under the command of Captain Dow and en route for Malta after disembarking troops on the island of Mudros during the Gallipoli Campaign, a periscope was spotted followed by the wakes of two torpedoes. A quick manoeuvre ensured that one weapon missed her by 30ft and the other by a mere 5! To have been sunk in such a fashion would have repeated her sister's fate when she was sunk by a single torpedo. The *Lusitania* is shown in dry dock in Liverpool before her trials. (Institute of Mechanical Engineers)

The *Mauretania* had been experiencing problems with her engines and thousands of turbine blades had to be replaced during her early 1914 refit. In the era before the common use of oxy-acetylene, the gases used for this work included compressed coal gas and, because of an incorrectly marked bottle, one of these containers exploded, instantly killing two Fitters and a ship's Engineer and seriously injuring seven others, one of whom later died in hospital.

A second event during the Great War occurred in the early hours of the following morning after the torpedo attack when, with no lights showing on either ship until the last minute, the *Mauretania* (illustrated in her guise as a troopship) was unable to avoid a collision with a small 3,994grt cargo vessel, the *Cardiff Hall*. The latter ship suffered severe damage to her bows, while the troopship sustained only slight damage to her starboard side-plating below her aft funnel.

After being released from Government service and after piecemeal renovations, the Cunarder re-entered the Atlantic Ferry. Although her turbines were in need of thorough overhaul after the neglect of the war years, she still managed good speeds during her voyages and there was still no other vessel to challenge her record. She carried on – almost wearily – under the command of Captain Rostron until, on 21 July 1921, a cry of 'Fire!' echoed around the dock. A workman had started a blaze while cleaning a carpet on 'E'-deck and it soon took hold. After several hours it was brought under control. (The picture shows one of several Firemen who were treated for smoke inhalation, etc.) It was decided to send her back to her builders at Newcastle for repair and reconstruction of affected staterooms, and a major decision was taken to seize the opportunity and convert her to oil fuel. This would enhance her efficiency and increase her speed, giving her a fighting chance against modern oil-fuelled competitors.

The *Mauretania*'s turbines had been well used during the Great War and were in desperate need of maintenance. The Southampton shipyard of John I. Thornycroft took her in hand in November 1923 to undertake this work and to make further improvements on the ship such as glazing in the forward part of 'B'-deck to make that area usable in bad weather. This extremely rare photograph shows work being undertaken on a turbine rotor. The turbine renovations had been almost complete when the shipyard's workforce went on strike demanding the restitution of the 10s (50p) war bonus that they had been receiving. (Vosper Thornycroft, Shipbuilders)

The liner was idle for two months when it was decided to tow her to Cherbourg for the completion of the work. During the journey the tow was lost and the drifting *Mauretania* was in danger of being blown ashore. Finally rescued, the work was completed and the ship returned home to greater triumphs.

The rescued clamber up the side of the huge vessel.

Over her lifetime, the *Mauretania* went to the rescue of three ships in distress, one before and two after the Great War. On 2 September 1910, the *Mauretania* (under Captain William 'Bowler Bill' Turner) went to the aid of the burning British steamer *West Point* (3,075 net tons) and picked up the sunken ship's survivors (including a kitten) from their lifeboat in appalling weather by providing a lee. The second was when she was in the charge of Captain Arthur Rostron, who had commanded the *Carpathia* during the rescue of 705 survivors from the *Titanic* in 1912. Now it was his turn to take the bigger ship to the rescue of the smaller when, on 30 March 1926, after experiencing damaging rough weather herself, the *Mauretania* received an SOS from the grain-carrying SS *Laleham* that was in a sinking condition after taking on a list in the bad weather. Captain Rostron put his ship into rescue mode and the liner even made 29 knots for an hour in her rescue bid. The grain ship's Captain and crew were, however, rescued by another vessel before the Cunarder reached the radioed position. On 19 November 1930, under Captain S.G.S. McNeil, the liner was again summoned to assist another cargo vessel, the Swedish *Ovidia* (3,343grt), which was in a sinking condition because of shifted cargo. Among the rescued was yet another cat!

GALAS, GALLANTRY AND THE GREAT WAR

Great ships experience great occasions and the *Mauretania* was certainly no exception. With the reputation of being the biggest ship in the world when she appeared – and certainly the fastest – her presence, like any great personality, was sought and feted for many a momentous occasion.

Her grandest moment was perhaps her launch but that was soon followed by her capturing the Blue Ribband from her sister, which had previously dashed Teutonic ambition.

Being the biggest and the fastest led to expectations that she would do something different, something mould-breaking, that she would excel. Big liners making a crossing either west or east spent several days in port being re-coaled and re-provisioned, the crew (if not required on board) having those days to spend ashore. But what if, instead of making a complete voyage in sixteen to eighteen days, that same voyage could be made in twelve? Cunard, through the reputation of the *Mauretania*, sought to achieve this grand publicity coup and what better season to make this gesture than Christmas, when mail, cargo and goodwill was at a premium?

Excitement built through newspaper coverage and this record voyage would be made in the spotlight of maximum publicity. Well-advertised, this 'Christmas Special' – 'one of the most remarkable in the history of the world' as the *New York Times* described it – left Liverpool under the command of Captain William Turner on 10 December 1910. However, Mother Nature stepped in and the westward crossing was bedevilled by appalling weather. In spite of this she rammed her way over at an average speed of 24.95 knots, arriving half a day late in New York. This delay meant an even speedier turn-around, which was admirably achieved by staff both on board and ashore, the latter having been massively increased in number.

The 'Christmas Dash' of December 1910 was surrounded by much publicity and 'what ifs', which included the potential use of the two sisters, *Mauretania* and *Lusitania*, as high-speed carriers of 6,000 vital tons of grain in time of war. The illustration above (taken from *The Graphic*) shows the *Mauretania* in this role under the speedy protection of one of the new fast, Invincible-class battlecruisers, the first of which was commissioned in 1908. This was a 'light' battleship (devised by that indomitable admiral, 'Jacky' Fisher) with less armour than a Dreadnought battleship to give a higher speed of 32 knots. The *Mauretania* was scheduled to make a similar voyage in 1911 but, because of a grounding in the River Mersey that caused buckling to eighty bottom plates, her sister took her place.

A crowning glory came to the *Mauretania* on 11 July 1913 when, as a part of a fleet of thirty-five merchant vessels and naval guardships assembled on the Mersey to mark the opening of the new Gladstone Dock, she was boarded and inspected by King George V, Queen Mary and Prince Albert. The illustration above shows the King almost reluctantly inspecting a troop of Firemen, mostly disregarded and often dismissed as uncouth but essential to the ship's operation. Cunard Commodore William Turner, dressed in his uniform of a Commander of the Royal Naval Reserve, can be seen above the King's left shoulder. After taking tea, the royal party then re-boarded the temporary Royal Yacht *Galatea* to open the new facility.

War came to the *Mauretania* as she was en route to New York. A signal that war had been declared between Great Britain and Germany was received at 1.30 a.m. on 5 August 1914. The liner immediately changed course and headed for Halifax, Nova Scotia, where she arrived the next morning. (Collection of Eric K. Longo)

The liner soon returned to Britain, where she was laid up, but *Lusitania* kept to an advertised transatlantic passenger schedule. This photograph, taken from HMS *Caronia* (a Cunarder that had been taken up by the Admiralty as an AMC that had been patrolling outside American territorial waters to prevent the escape of German vessels) just after the liners had exchanged mails, might be the last picture taken of the *Lusitania*. She was hit by a torpedo five days later on 7 May 1915, fired from the German submarine *U-20*. Sinking in just eighteen minutes, she took 1,198 passengers and crew with her – including 128 neutral American citizens, an act that the United States would remember with a vengeance two years later.

The *Mauretania*'s second deployment was to bring those many troops who had either been wounded or fallen sick back to Britain. The latter category of invalids was in the majority as the hot, fly-infested unsanitary conditions of the Dardanelles were ideal for spreading dysentery. For this work the *Mauretania* was painted white with buff funnels and, around her hull, a broad green line was painted interspersed with large red crosses to denote her status as a hospital ship. Fitted to accommodate 2,500 patients, she initially sailed from Liverpool but transferred to Southampton as this port involved a shorter journey home and was near to the great Victorian military hospital at Netley. This postcard shows her sailing down Southampton Water and copies were sold by patients to raise funds. Apparently buying two cards, this sender's message on the reverse, although sympathetic, was unfortunately somewhat ambiguous in a darkly humorous way (the emphasis is mine): 'This is a card Tom bought from a poor soldier in Netley Hospital who has *lost both legs in the war, so I thought that you would like one each.*'

In accordance with the Geneva Convention (hence the Red Cross being an 'inverted' version of the Swiss Flag), the *Mauretania*'s hospital ship markings were brightly illuminated at night to identify her mission of mercy. She would also make three voyages as HMHS *Mauretania*, bringing back a total of 6,298 patients attended by 2,307 medical staff. The ship was laid up on 21 May 1916 after her third mission.

After three months of idleness she was again called into service, this time as a troopship, to bring 6,214 Dominion troops from the Canadian port of Halifax to Liverpool. She made only one such voyage, between October and November 1916. Men are seen in this photograph busily painting her prow while in the Haligonian city. (Collection of Eric K. Longo)

After that single voyage to Nova Scotia, the *Mauretania* was laid up at Greenock until March 1918, when she was chartered as a transport to bring American 'Doughboys' to Britain, transporting in seven voyages a total of 33,610 GIs. For this work she was painted in the first of two 'dazzle' schemes, using long sweeping curves and devised to confuse enemy submarines on her course, size and even identity. (Photograph courtesy Eric Sauder)

The second dazzle scheme was executed in straighter geometric patterns. In both schemes port and starboard patterns were of a different design.

Whilst on these GI shuttles, the *Mauretania* made Liverpool her home. The troops were taken to training camps, such as the nearby establishment at Knotty Ash, for further training. (Collection of Günter Bäbler)

At war's end the *Mauretania* was employed in repatriating the American troops that she had brought over. Leaving Liverpool on 25 November 1918, she arrived in New York Harbor to a tumultuous welcome on 2 December. The three tall posts seen near to the stern were booms fitted on both sides and were normally used on warships to tether ship's boats away from the side and provide access to the mothership via Jacob's ladders. On the *Mauretania* they would have been lowered about a hinge and used to evacuate the ship in the event of an emergency. What the wildly cheering spectators and those on the whistle-blowing tugs did not realise – but the soldiers did – was that the troops, bemused by their welcome home, had gone over on the 'Maury' (aka 'Mary'), had been taken to a camp near Liverpool, been given an overseas postings medal, and returned on the *Mauretania* as soon as she was ready – all without them having seen combat! Illustration from a lantern slide.

During this charter she was laid up during September and October, which was probably when her dazzle was overpainted with sombre grey. February 1919 saw her final repatriation trip to New York, departing from Southampton. She is seen here entering the Outer Harbor to a tumultuous welcome (note the various aircraft).

March 1919 saw another Southampton departure, but this one was bound for Halifax with 3,946 Canadian troops. The *Mauretania*'s war came to an end on 27 May 1919 after four years of excellent service, during which she had carried 10,391 troops as a troopship, 8,605 wounded and medical staff as a hospital ship, and 69,751 troops as a transport.

CAPTAINS, CREW AND 'CARGO'

The many thousands of people who travelled on the *Mauretania*, whether as crew or as passengers (the 'cargo', as the crew often referred to their charges), ensured that a cross-section of humanity was seen on board. The crew used the ship as a means of livelihood, while the passengers naturally came from all walks of life and had a myriad of reasons for crossing the North Atlantic as, in those days before jet airliners took hold in the late 1950s, travelling by ship was, indeed, the only way to cross. Some (mostly the well-to-do) travelled for pleasure (although in midwinter there might have been few of those), while others travelled for business or political reasons. But the majority (the poor) in the early days were making a one-way journey of emigration to a hopefully new life in a land that, at the time, needed them and their labour as they made their escape from persecution (both religious and political), escape from poverty, escape from war and revolution, etc., all hoping that the golden door of new opportunity overseen by the Statue of Liberty would open to success and, remotely possible, riches.

As the liner was based in Liverpool (the name that appeared curving under her stern as her port of registration), most of her crew came from that area and many were Liverpool Irish. That section of the community had arrived from Ireland – perhaps fleeing their own poverty or descended from the victims of the Irish Potato Famine (The Great Starvation) of 1845–49. As the Irish ferry terminated at Liverpool, many of its passengers had ceased their journey of exile and made their home in the maritime city, many hundreds subsequently seeking work on the ships that plied from the port – usually in the boiler rooms with its attendant back-breaking toil. As a result, the men who took up this hard work had the reputation of being tough, hard fighting and hard drinking (hardly surprising as on-board discipline and conditions were harsh and alcohol was generally prohibited).

Officers came from all parts of the country, having trained on one of the famed training (or school) ships – decommissioned sailing warships such as the *Conway* (ex-HMS *Nile*) on the River Mersey off Rock Ferry or the *Worcester* on the Thames. Following training the cadets would then serve five years at sea on a sailing ship, all the while studying to pass examinations in order to achieve higher rank until finally getting their 'ticket' – their qualification to hold their own command. Cunard's officers all had their Masters' Tickets but still had to join the company as navigating officers with the ambition of becoming one of the company's often highly regarded skippers.

One of several training vessels in the country, the *Wellesley* (ex-HMS *Boscawen*) had been established on the River Tyne for 13- to 16-year-old waifs and strays from Newcastle and, later, further cities further afield. It was anticipated that these 'saved' would then join the Royal or Merchant Navies. The old ship was damaged by fire in 1914 so, to provide a 'proper' training, the Shipping Federation established a Sea School at Gravesend, a more formal training establishment, in 1918 for boys aged 16 to 18 who wished to pursue a life at sea in Britain's Merchant Navy either as deck crew or in the victualling (hotel) department. To this effect, the school acquired the sailing vessel *Arranmore* in 1921 and renamed her *Vindicatrix* (later moved to Sharpness). Once employed on passenger ships, the boys who joined the victualling department referred to 'the cargo' (their passengers) as being either 'good bloods' or 'bad bloods', depending on their ability to tip and the size of the gratuity. These tips found their way down through the ship, e.g. a tip given to a bedroom steward was proportioned to those who supplied him with the materials with which to do his job (i.e. laundry services to ensure that tablecloths, cutlery, crockery and napkins, etc., were available on time), and dining room staff made payments to galleys for promptly delivered food.

The very first Captain of the *Mauretania* was Welshman Captain John Pritchard (see Episode 8) and the last was Captain A.T. Brown, who commanded her on her final, one-way journey to Rosyth in 1935 (see Episode 14). The longest-serving Captain – and perhaps the one who loved her the most – was Captain Arthur Henry Rostron. Later knighted, he had superbly organised an earlier command, the little *Carpathia*, to make an urgent dash to rescue the survivors from the wreck of the White Star liner *Titanic* in April 1912. (Frontispiece from *Home From the Sea* by Captain Sir A.H. Rostron)

Clockwise from left: It was not often that a Chief Engineer made the limelight but here Andrew Cockburn poses smartly with Captain 'Sandy' McNeil at the end of a record voyage in August 1929. (Illustration from *In Great Waters: Memoirs of a Master Mariner* by Captain S.G.S. McNeil)

The last Captain of the liner during her final days of Atlantic service was Captain Reginald Peel. (*The Sphere*, 13 April 1935)

Other men who served on the ship had the same standing as the Captain and wore four gold rings on their sleeves. Later, after the loss of the *Titanic*, they wore purple bands separating the gold bands in a tribute to the engineers of the *Titanic* who had perished to a man. These were the ship's Chief Engineers, the first of whom was John Currie (seated front, fourth from right, wearing four stripes) with his staff of twenty-eight Senior and Junior Engineers. These officers would be in charge of large Engine and Boiler Room staffs of 76 Greasers, 202 Firemen and 121 Trimmers.

Between her maiden voyage and her last, sad journey the *Mauretania* had ten Captains.

Commanders
RMS *Mauretania*

1907–09	Captain John T. Pritchard
1910–14	Captain William T. Turner
1914	Captain Sir James Charles
The Great War	
(1914–1918)	Captain Sir James Charles
	Captain Daniel Dow
	Captain J.C. Barr
	Captain Sir Arthur H. Rostron
1918–26	Captain Sir Arthur H. Rostron
1926–27	Captain E.G. Diggle
1928–31	Captain Samuel G.S. McNeil
1931–34	Captain R.V. Peel
1935*	Captain A.T. Brown

*Single trip

During her lifetime the running of the *Mauretania*'s Engine and Boiler Rooms were supervised by nine Chief Engineers. The longest serving was Andrew Cockburn with twelve remarkable years, during which the liner was rejuvenated after her wearying war service and her following conversion to oil fuel. Mr Cockburn, from Kelso in Scotland, had had an eventful career, having been Senior Second Engineer on board the *Lusitania* when she had been torpedoed and sunk in May 1915. The Chief on that fateful uncompleted crossing had been Archie Bryce; Captain Turner was said to have wept when he saw his Chief's recovered body in Queenstown.

Chief Engineers
RMS *Mauretania*

1907–10	J. Currie
1910–12	J. Kendal
1912–16	J. Carruthers
1916–18	A. Allan
1918–19	J. McDonald
1919–32	A. Cockburn
1932–33	E. Barton
1933–34	W. Sutcliffe
1935*	H. Bolling

*Single trip

The forty-two deck crew of the ship included Seamen, Able-Bodied Seamen and Boatswains. Here a group of passengers – well wrapped up for an Atlantic crossing – have asked Able-Bodied (AB) Seaman Archibald Weir of Grove Road, Southampton, to pose with them for a souvenir photograph. (Family collection of Roy Bennet)

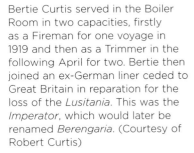

Bertie Curtis served in the Boiler Room in two capacities, firstly as a Fireman for one voyage in 1919 and then as a Trimmer in the following April for two. Bertie then joined an ex-German liner ceded to Great Britain in reparation for the loss of the *Lusitania*. This was the *Imperator*, which would later be renamed *Berengaria*. (Courtesy of Robert Curtis)

Chief Pantry Man Matthew Mooney (right) has a quiet smoke and an amiable chat with a fellow crew member. (Courtesy of Zac Coles)

Bell boys joined the ship at 14 years of age and had to purchase their own uniforms, including three 'whites' for cruising. John Jenkins of Portsmouth was one of these. Woken at 5.30 a.m. by the 'Glory Hole' steward (known as a 'Peggy'), cleaning duties were undertaken before breakfast and he spent the rest of the day attending to passengers' needs, such as opening large glass doors for them (tips were good – one lad on the later Queen liners asked to leave the ship as he was getting too much money!). Free newspapers were supplied for passengers in New York who, unaware of this service, were charged full price for them by a canny young Jenkins! Prior to sailing, John had to walk around the decks sounding a gong and calling the final notice that the ship was about to sail: 'All visitors ashore! All visitors ashore!' (By kind permission of Robert Hind)

Musicians (bandsmen) were not employed directly by the shipping company but were contracted by an agency ashore, such as Black's of Liverpool. However, they had to sign the ship's articles and were given 'free' accommodation and meals, and were paid a nominal 1s a month. Wallace Hartley was a one-time Bandmaster on the *Mauretania* before transferring to the White Star Line. He would go on to achieve immortal fame leading his band playing as the *Titanic* sank beneath their feet. All of that ship's musicians perished. A pianist on board the *Mauretania* before the Great War was Jack MaCann, pictured here. (By kind permission of Clare Blakey)

The smallest member of the ship's crew! Captain Rostron's cat and her kittens.

Travelling in 1920 – and without a hint of the radical fashions that were about to take the world by storm – passenger Madame Luisa Tetrazzini looks every inch a bel canto diva, complete with a less-warlike version of Brunhild's winged helmet! A charismatic and brilliant singer of her day, she had duetted and written a book with the great Enrico Caruso as well as penning her own volumes, *My Life of Song* and *How to Sing*. As with other great singers, she gave her name to a dish, Chicken Tetrazzini, and, in later life, said, 'I am old, I am fat, but I am still Tetrazzini.' What a woman!

Many politicians and businessmen took the *Mauretania* if they required a fast passage across the North Atlantic. Such a person who had embraced both posts was a remarkable man with a remarkable career, Sir Eric Geddes CCB CBE PC (photographed on board on 8 May 1925). His career had covered jobs from lumberjack, steel worker, railway station master, and builder of light railways in India. On return to Britain he became Deputy General Manager of the North Eastern Railway. In the Great War he was appointed Minister of Munitions, greatly improving the desperate shortfalls in the supply at the front. He became a Member of Parliament in 1917 in order to enable him to become First Lord of the Admiralty. Two years later he became Minister of Transport, in which post he greatly reduced public spending in what became known as the Geddes Axe. In 1922 he resigned from politics and entered industry as a Director of Dunlop Rubber as well as Chairman of Imperial Airways.

Rich and famous together walked the pristine decks of the *Mauretania*. Here 20-year-old socialite Miss Isabel Rockefeller (granddaughter of Standard Oil's co-founder William Rockefeller) is captured on camera as she returns from a cruise in April 1922.

One of the wealthiest men to travel on the *Mauretania* was John Pierpont Morgan (Jr), son of J.P. Morgan, whose International Mercantile Marine had almost bought Cunard at the beginning of the century. After making a further fortune as the purchaser of munitions and supplies for Britain and France during the Great War, Morgan Jr then lent vast sums to Germany and other European countries after the war. His only complaint of travelling on the *Mauretania* seems to be about a yapping dog in the next cabin!

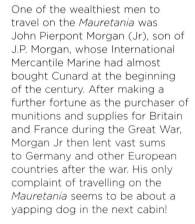

Being seen on the fastest ship in the world was a 'must do' – especially if you were a star of the silver screen – and Oriel Ross was no exception. Born Muriel Swinstead (a few months before the *Mauretania* made her maiden voyage), she was multi-talented, being an actress on both stage and screen, a dancer (stage and cabaret) and an artist. As a dancer she had appeared in legendary ballet director Sergei Diaghilev's *Ballet Ode*. Among the many films in which she appeared was the British drama *Self Made Lady*. As an amateur artist, Ross lived for some time in the gregarious Epstein house in London. Even when she was on board ship she could not resist picking up her pencil ... even making this line drawing of one of the liner's chefs!

CRUISING TO THE END

By the early 1930s the *Mauretania* was wearing out. She had been pushed through everything that the North Atlantic could throw at her and, in her final days of glory, had made an outstanding effort in attempting to regain her record lost in 1929. However, the oft-tempestuous ocean, with the reputation of being the roughest in the world, had taken its toll. Subsequent dry-dockings began to paint a bleak future for the still-popular and beloved old ship, by now dubbed 'The Grand Old Lady of the North Atlantic'.

A huge, new Cunarder was being planned (initial proposals being mooted in 1927) with the possibility of a sister to follow. These two ships would take over the express service previously maintained by three – *Mauretania*, *Aquitania* and *Berengaria* – all of which were becoming elderly.

In November 1922 Cunard tried its hand at long-distance cruising and sent the 19,695grt *Laconia* on a world cruise, the first by any ship. This liner had been delivered to Cunard in January of the previous year (1921) by her builders, Swan Hunter & Wigham Richardson, who had famously built the *Mauretania*. This historic cruise by the *Laconia* was suitably ambitious as the liner circumnavigated the globe, a journey that took 130 days with twenty-two ports of call – and it set the precedent for the century to follow.

Like as waves make towards the pebbled shore,
So do our lives hasten to their end.

'Sonnet 60', William Shakespeare

The *Mauretania*'s first cruise (a Winter one 'of unprecedented interest') was on a special charter by American Express and took her to Alexandria in Egypt via several romantic and exotic ports. She left New York on 10 February 1923 with prices from $950 (First Class only). The *Laconia* had left New York on 21 November 1922 and advertised that her passengers would be travelling 30,000 miles by land and by sea in 130 days. The fabled tomb of Egyptian Pharaoh Tutankhamun had been discovered on 4 November 1922 and its excavation proved a great attraction for the wealthy travellers. The ship's sixth and final Mediterranean cruise took place in 1930; a planned seventh would be cancelled due to the Great Depression. Here, in one of her following more affordable cruises, and in a delightfully candid snapshot, Captain McNeil takes a moment to cheerfully socialise with 'Father'. (Private collection)

To regain lost revenue, along with many others, the ship was put into affordable Caribbean cruises during the lengthy time of lay-up in between crossings (cabin prices for these were also reduced drastically), with the added attraction that the *Mauretania*'s greater speed enabled her to perform longer sorties. She was also able to give her passengers the thrill of her legendary speed – but in calmer waters than those of the North Atlantic! These long-weekend cruises took in Bermuda and Halifax, while, later, longer ones ventured to Havana, Cuba, where large crowds assembled to watch her initial arrival and departure. (Collection of Charles Haas and John Eaton)

Cruising passengers were offered a variety of 1930s entertainment, which filled whole days as soon as she left port. Cruisers could take tea in the Verandah (the ubiquitous potted palms also appeared in the Dining Saloon) ...

... then dance in the evenings (note the band on the balcony) on the beautifully sprung parquet dance floor that had been fitted in the Lounge during the major refit and repairs of 1921 after the fire and her conversion to oil fuel.

By painting the *Mauretania* white (in 1933), it was found that her interior temperatures could be reduced by up to 9°F, while her boot-topping (below the waterline) was painted green. When she left Southampton in her new livery an old observer reportedly remarked that she looked like 'a bloomin' wedding cake!' She made two rare cruises from Southampton in April and May 1932, first to Casablanca and then to Madeira, both calling into the British Overseas Territory of Gibraltar to give her travellers a feel of home (even though they were on the ship to get away from it!), but with the difference of seasonably warmer sunshine. (*Shipbuilding and Shipping Record*, 8 June 1933)

Her first departure in a series of five twelve-and-a half-day cruises as 'Britain's White Speed Queen' left New York on 8 July 1933. Here she passes the H&M (Hudson & Manhattan) Railroad building on Church Street in Lower Manhattan to port. (Ambrose Greenway Collection)

Off-duty crew enjoyed themselves in their on-board pub, The Pig and Whistle. Here the ship's band sometimes played for their colleagues in the austere, undecorated room.

The *Mauretania*, sparklingly resplendent in her white livery, anchored at one of her ports of call but ...

... she had to return to Southampton for thorough maintenance periods and is seen here raised in the Floating Dock that had been opened by the Prince of Wales. It appears that a lady sightseer has been allowed on to the dock bottom – something that would not be allowed in these days of health and safety!

The great Cunarder being manoeuvred by the submerged Floating Dock at Southampton. It can be seen that the *Mauretania* has canvas covers over her middle two funnels to prevent ingression of inclement weather.

Deck sports enjoyed in the increasing sunshine involved deck tennis (played with large rubber rings) and shuffle board on the Boat Deck, as well as ...

Part of the entertainment was provided by members of the *Mauretania* Social and Athletics Club. A successful football team of crew members called itself the 'Maries' and a cricket team won a 9-carat gold medal in 1910 presented by grocery baron Sir Thomas Lipton, who travelled on the liner. The crew also put on afternoon boxing matches of three rounds each of two minutes. Contestants such as Cyclone Peers ('the Widnes Marvel'), Battling Hussey ('the Liverpool Wonder'), Kid Booth, and Boy Bigley would slog it out to the delight of the spectators – including socialising officers!

... swimming in a small and often leaky crowded temporary pool constructed from wood and canvas and filled with seawater.

One man – and his small team – ensured that the passengers enjoyed themselves with a full programme of daily events: the figure in a white suit on the Bridge wing is probably Howard L. Greene, Cruise Director for American Express.

This wonderful photograph of the *Mauretania* at one of her destinations shows that she is at anchor as she has a single black ball raised above her Docking Bridge platform. Wind scoops project out from some of her ports (she was not air-conditioned other than for punkah-louvres in cabin ventilation trunks). Of special note are the eye-bolts under her counter that assisted when removing propellers. A chef and two friends chat on the taffrail.

Definitely not acceptable in these enlightened days of animal rights but an on-board 'sport' in the temperate zones of the Caribbean in the 1930s was turtle racing, although the unfortunate creatures first had to escape their box! The passengers enjoyed the race meeting, and probably had a few 'bob' bet on the hapless animals.

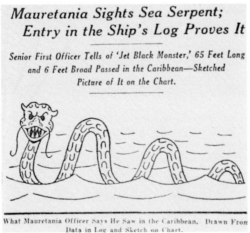

Mauretania Sights Sea Serpent; Entry in the Ship's Log Proves It

Senior First Officer Tells of 'Jet Black Monster,' 65 Feet Long and 6 Feet Broad Passed in the Caribbean—Sketched Picture of It on the Chart.

What Mauretania Officer Says He Saw in the Caribbean. Drawn From Data in Log and Sketch on Chart.

One creature that the passengers would not have cared to see too closely was this 'sea monster' espied from the Bridge. The Captain, who had not seen the animal but trusted his officers' word, ordered the occurrence to be entered in the Official Log along with a drawing and a note that it had been black and about 45ft long. Under the Merchant Shipping Act of 1894 Section 239 (6) the Master signed the entry, which could be 'admissible in evidence'. None other than the very respectable Captain Rostron had also seen one of these creatures when Chief Officer on the old *Campania* in 1911.

On 26 September 1934 the *Mauretania* left New York, ostensibly for dry-docking and maintenance in Southampton, during which crossing she still managed a creditable 24.4 knots. That very same day, Yard No. 534, a huge new liner that had been built for the by-now amalgamated Cunard and White Star North Atlantic lines, was launched at the Clydebank shipyard of John Brown, her number being replaced in a surprise naming as *Queen Mary*. However, on arrival in Southampton the *Mauretania* was laid up awaiting a maintenance that would never materialise. She was joined by the *Olympic* on the following 12 April (a funnel of which can be seen behind the seaman to the left) but, ten days before this, it was announced that the beloved '*Maury*' was to be sold for breaking up. At an on-board auction that lasted from Tuesday, 14 May until the Friday, the liner's fittings were sold in 3,503 lots (nearly 20,000 items). The ship was then readied for her journey north to the shipbreaking dock of Metal Industries Ltd in Rosyth Dockyard, for which a special banner was made that would be flown from the ship and stated the years between which the *Mauretania* had held the Blue Ribband – 1907–29. Because the banner was of a blue material, many misinformed reports stated that it was the Blue Ribband itself!

Prior to her departure, 40ft had to be removed from her mast tips to enable her to pass under the Forth Railway Bridge. By 9 p.m. on 1 July 1935, thousands of erstwhile 'mourners' had gathered on the quayside to bid a final farewell to their beloved *Mauretania*. As daylight dimmed, the old liner, in her now rust-streaked white livery and with a few lights on to defeat the falling dusk, the old ship was assisted out of her berth into the River Test – taking care not to collide with the *Olympic* that now lay ahead of her – where she was turned to face downstream towards Southampton Water, all to the strains of 'Auld Lang Syne'.

Sixty-five guests and a skeleton crew boarded for the journey up the east coast of England. The journey would be a slow one as she only had fuel enough to get her to her destination. As she steamed northwards, hundreds of people, recalling the pride that they had felt in the *Mauretania*'s achievements (even if they hadn't previously seen her), flocked to the coast to see her pass. At 10 p.m. on 2 July she slowed off Scarborough as her master, Captain Brown, lived there, and a decision was made at the last minute to accede to a request that she also pause by the River Tyne where she had been built. All Tyneside seemed to turn out to emotionally – tearfully, in many cases – bid her a last goodbye before she once again, accompanied by a few craft full of spectators, moved on. This evocative photograph shows her off Longsands off Tynemouth as she starts to move north after her thirty-minute tribute to the town and its people that had built her.

By the early morning of 4 July the *Mauretania* had reached her destination and Scots piper Adam MacGillvray played a lament as she was edged through the main lock entrance and into Rosyth's outer basin. (Collection of Eric K. Longo)

EPISODES IN COLOUR

Travellers on the ferries crossing the River Tyne from Newcastle or Shields would see the still-incomplete liner as she rose from the slipway and, as she did so, they made a place in their hearts for her until she universally became 'The Pride of the Tyne'. This postcard, giving a rather too imaginative impression of the ship as she might appear, was sold both as a souvenir and as an advertisement for the ferry company.

The day the *Mauretania* went to sea for the first time to conduct her Preliminary (Builder's) Trials – 17 September 1907 – was made a holiday on Tyneside. Thousands watched her from ashore and afloat as, still painted in the grey of her launch day (and now rather weather-worn), she progressed down the river to the open sea accompanied by pleasure craft of all sizes and resounding cheers, to which she replied with blasts from her whistles. Surrounded by the faster of the accompanying craft, the liner approaches the two piers that protect Tynemouth from the worst of the storms that blow in from the North Sea. Two lighthouses stand side by side on the North Pier, the smaller of which would soon be demolished after it and the old North Pier had been severely damaged in a storm ten years previously.

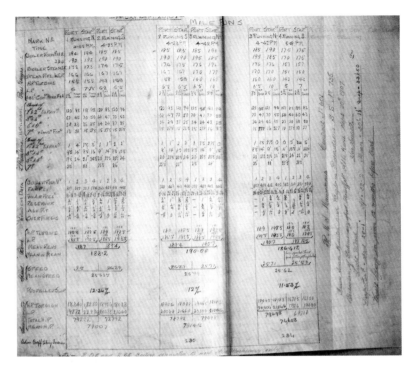

Clockwise from above: The *Mauretania* returned to builders Swan Hunter & Wigham Richardson of Wallsend for her final fitting out, painting and some remedial work to obviate vibration that had been experienced at some time during her trials. The day 22 October was another gala day on Tyneside as she was leaving the river for the last time bound for Liverpool and her contractors' trials and acceptance.

The new liner was trialled off the east coast from Whitley Bay to St Abb's Head, where she turned to repeat her course; this double run considered the flow of tide to give an average for both runs. These trials took four days with measurements and readings being taken from all over the ship. According to this sample page (this and subsequent pages hitherto unpublished), she averaged almost 26 knots on this particular day, 20 September, a fantastic result that comfortably exceeded her contract speed – and this was after a year afloat during which time her hull bottom had become fouled with marine growth and with some launching gear still attached! The choice of revolutionary turbines as her (and her sister's) propulsors had indeed been vindicated.

In command of the ship was Captain John Pritchard, a Welshman with a lifetime of experience at sea. This portrait of the Captain was commissioned shortly after he took the *Mauretania* to sea. (Estate of Captain John Pritchard, now in the possession of Museums on Merseyside)

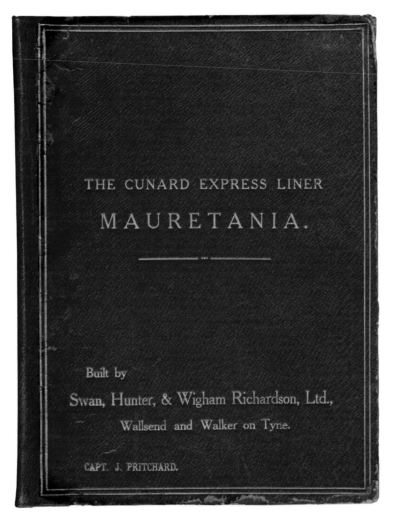

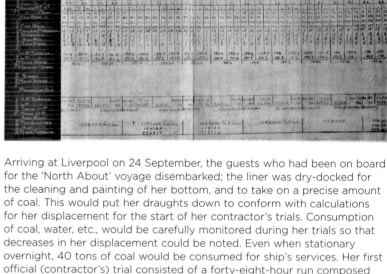

Arriving at Liverpool on 24 September, the guests who had been on board for the 'North About' voyage disembarked; the liner was dry-docked for the cleaning and painting of her bottom, and to take on a precise amount of coal. This would put her draughts down to conform with calculations for her displacement for the start of her contractor's trials. Consumption of coal, water, etc., would be carefully monitored during her trials so that decreases in her displacement could be noted. Even when stationary overnight, 40 tons of coal would be consumed for ship's services. Her first official (contractor's) trial consisted of a forty-eight-hour run composed of two continuous sets of runs from Corswall Point to the Longships Lighthouse, each run being of 304 miles; the total of over 1,200 miles represented sailing halfway across the Atlantic.

Many presentations were made on that historic day of departure, not least of which was one of a silver tea and coffee set to the Captain and, later, a red leatherette-bound and gold-embossed copy of a special edition of the technically informed *Shipbuilder* magazine. Captain Pritchard would make good and well-thumbed use of his copy in the months to come. (Estate of Captain John Pritchard, author's collection)

A summary – or abstract – sheet was prepared of the ship's overall performance for the forty-eight-hour endurance trial through the Irish Sea and this showed that on her second set of runs she averaged 26.315 knots, having achieved a magnificent 27.367 knots on the last southward run.

Following the endurance trials, speed trials were then run, the first over the Skelmorlie Measured Mile off Wemyss Bay, and the second between Holy Island and Ailsa Craig, on which she averaged nearly 27 knots. This beautifully hand-printed linen sheet provides an abstract of the trial results. The illustration on page 85 gives a wonderful impression of her at speed on this course. The results for 6 November are recorded on another hand-printed sheet of blue-finished linen. Her performance during the trials between Ailsa Craig and Holy Island exceeded expectations, with an average speed of 26.17 knots.

TWENTY-TWO TRAINS, OF THIRTY TRUCKS, EACH TRUCK CONTAINING 10 TONS, ARE NECESSARY TO CARRY THE COAL REQUIRED FOR ONE TRIP BETWEEN LIVERPOOL AND NEW YORK.

A tinted glass lantern slide demonstrates the quantity of superior 'Best Welsh' steam coal required for each westward crossing of the North Atlantic, including a day's margin in case of delay through bad weather etc. (her bunkers would be replenished with American coals in New York). The illustration shows twenty-two trains of thirty wagons each carrying 10 tons of coal. The coal was mined from a pit owned by the Ocean (Merthyr) Steam Coal Company, which produced 9,500 tons a day, the output being solely reserved for Admiralty trials, the Royal Yachts and for both the *Mauretania* and *Lusitania*.

Judging from the amount of interest that the liner is eliciting, this is the *Mauretania* after her maiden arrival in New York, with derricks busily fussing over the forward open hatch. The postcard's sender, Nelly, writes cryptically, 'We are waiting for four bells [2 p.m.] afternoon watch.' (Collection of Charles Haas and John P. Eaton)

A corner of the Louis Seize-style lounge that demonstrates the quality of the workmanship. Cross-veneered panels of rich mahogany with gilded decoration of ribbon-tied oak foliage and exquisitely carved columns with ormolu capitols and bases made the room 'unequalled in any steamship and rarely surpassed even in a palace'. The mantelpiece is of Brêche Violet marble. This room was purchased by Mr Ronald Avery (wine merchant of Bristol), when the ship's fittings were auctioned (Lots 254–301) prior to her being broken up and later formed part of the prestigious Mauretania Bar and Grill in Bristol.

Atmospheric as black-and-white photographs can be, they cannot always do justice to a subject's colouring but an artist's illustration can. This detailed contemporary drawing shows the Saloon (First) Class Lounge and Music Room (note the grand piano at the far end) decorated with beautifully carved and gilded panelling. Both wood and Fleur de Pêche marble columns and pilasters were designed by C. Mellier & Co. (as was the Library), a most distinguished and renowned London cabinetmaking firm. One of the three famous French tapestries at the far end of the room, cream Wilton carpet patterned in large leaf trellis and rosettes and matching curtains, and brocaded chairs in various colours contributed to brighten the prospect.

Framed in carved and gilded oak leaves, this recess shows the Cunard crest of a laurel-surrounded crowned lion rampant holding a globe. Again, this panel can be found in the Mauretania Bar, Bristol.

Another Mellier-designed room that vied with the Lounge as the most beautiful on the ship was the Library. *The Shipbuilder* described the panelling as being made from 'sycamore stained a silver grey'. However, the 1935 Auction catalogue described it differently ...

... when the 11ft-high panelling was listed in the sale catalogue as being in 'the Hepplewhite style, of polished harewood'. This timber was sometimes called 'airwood', a type of maple with a curled or 'fiddleback' figure, used to make the backs of musical stringed instruments. Of a natural off-white colour, it was stained for use on the ship with iron sulphate, producing the silver-grey tone as described in *The Shipbuilder*. However, in a relatively short time the harewood turned a rich brown. The publication continued its description of the panelling as being: 'quartered and mitred ... in acanthus framings, intercepted by uprights of pearled leaf medallions and paterae, friezes and mouldings of vitruvian scrolls, echinus ... all of carved gilt wood'. This splendid room was, as Lots 213–250, purchased by builder Mr Charles Boot and his partner Mr J. Arthur Rank and was later to become the restaurant (later boardroom) of new film studios planned at Iver Heath in Buckinghamshire. They also bid successfully for various cabins, intended to become dressing rooms.

Second Class were well looked after with this luxurious Drawing Room with various gilded maple woods used in its decor and a matching maple piano provided for entertainment. Crimson carpeting and velvet upholsteries set off the small, elegant tables, which were still bolted to the deck, although the chairs were free moving.

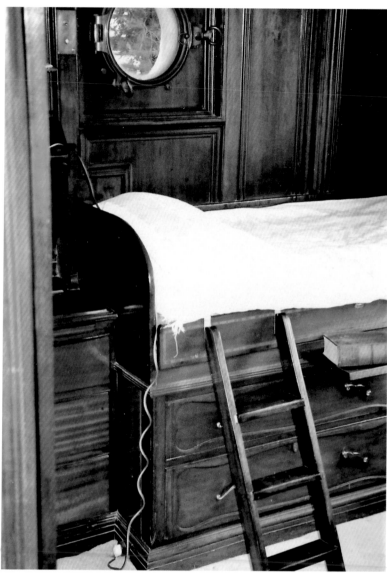

Clockwise from above: A corner of the Drawing Room amply demonstrated that the effort put into the decor of Second-Class accommodation did not fall far behind that put into First. Figured maple gave a light feeling to the room and the gilt, be-ribboned, reeded carving reflected the fasces of Roman justice (later, ominously, adopted as the symbol of a repressive political movement that bore its name).

A doorway with its rich carvings of ribbon-bound reeds, echinus 'egg-and-dart' and laurel swags.

Simpler decor was applied to the Captain's quarters, which, along with the Second-Class Drawing Room, now adorn a private residence near Poole, Dorset.

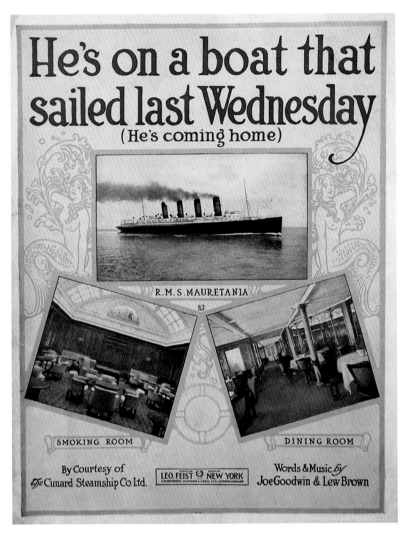

The famous liner was well known and her superbly decorated rooms proved equally so – they even adorned the cover of a piece of sheet music in the hope that the image association would boost sales!

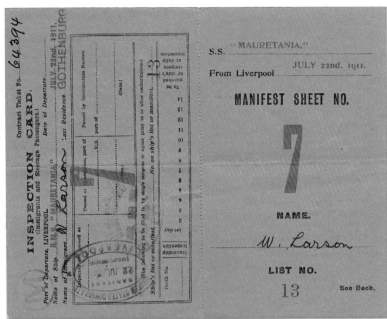

Much attention was paid to passengers travelling in the luxury of First Class, whereas those in Third Class travelling as 'immigrants and steerage passengers' – although well looked after on the *Mauretania* – were less cosseted. This document, almost an ID card (this one issued to a Swedish emigrant in 1911), was in two parts, one of which showed on which manifest the passenger was listed and had to be carried at all times. Precise instructions stated that one part had to be 'pinned to the coat or dress of the passenger in a prominent position', while the other part of the card declared that the passenger had been vaccinated and exhorted its possessor to 'Keep this card to avoid detention at Quarantine and on railroads in the United States'. Immigration drastically fell after the Great War, when strict immigrant quotas were introduced by the US in 1921 and 1924. The fall-off in this trade led to the creation of Tourist and Tourist Third that encouraged lower-income groups to travel abroad on holiday.

A wonderful evocation of the River Mersey by renowned artist Kenneth Denton Shoesmith. As a youngster Shoesmith was a cadet on the training ship *Conway*, an old decommissioned man-o'-war, from which he used to draw and paint the shipping on the river (it was said that the commanding officer allowed him time off to do so). In this wonderfully busy painting the horizon is completely obscured due to the amount of shipping on the river, which includes a battleship, HMS *Conway*, with its Captain looking down from a stern gallery, and the *Mauretania* as she arrives following an Atlantic crossing. The plume of smoke between the latter two ships discloses a subtle and barely visible patch of blue that reveals a vessel of the numerous fleet of Alfred Holt's Ocean Steam Ship Company – the Blue Funnel Line – known locally as 'The Birkenhead Navy'. A diminutive Mersey ferry steams to the liner's port side. (Collection of Ulster Folk and Transport Museum, National Museums NI)

The *Mauretania*'s home port of Liverpool was thriving and the floating Princes Landing Stage was built to facilitate the embarkation and disembarkation of passengers. It was also used as an observation platform for those who just wished to watch the activity on the river.

A view over Fishguard Bay as the *Mauretania* arrives for the first time on 30 August 1909. The small Welsh port had been chosen because of its sheltered position and depth of water, its redevelopment as a port by the Great Western Railway and its location – it was nearer to London than Liverpool – and would cut several hours off a passenger's journey to the metropolis or to the Continent.

S. S. CARPATHIA WHO RESCUED 705 SURVIVORS OF THE S. S. TITANIC

After the loss of the White Star liner *Titanic* on her maiden voyage in 1912, postcard companies rushed to issue commemorative cards. If a photograph of the lost ship was not available, pictures of other vessels were used to satisfy a public that probably did not know what the lost ship looked like. Step in *Mauretania*! Photographs of her were refashioned as the *Titanic*. But the smaller rescue ship, Cunard's *Carpathia*, posed another problem – until *Mauretania* was deprived of three funnels and the smaller ship's name was overprinted on her bow! (Collection of Günter Bäbler)

A portrait of Guglielmo Marconi, whose development of wireless assisted in the saving of the 705 survivors from the sinking of the *Titanic*. During the early stages of his experiments Marconi had often travelled in ships commanded by Captain Pritchard and had presented this framed autographed photograph to him in 1904 while travelling on the *Campania*. (Estate of Captain John Pritchard)

PROGRAMME
OF
ENTERTAINMENT
IN AID OF
SEAMEN'S CHARITIES AT LIVERPOOL & NEW YORK.

HELD ON BOARD THE
CUNARD R.M.S. "MAURETANIA"
By permission of CAPTAIN J. T. W. CHARLES, C.B., R.D., R.N.R.

ON WEDNESDAY EVENING, SEPT. 23rd, 1914,
In the Third Class Dining Saloon at 8 o'clock.

Chairman   -   -   -   MR. W. E. BRISTOL

❧ PART I. ❧

Pianoforte Solo	... Miss Irene O'Leary
Song	Mr. P. Dolan
Melodeon Selection	... Mr. G. Miller
Song	... Mr. J. W. Dodds
Recitation	... Mrs. G. A. Bjorkstron
Piccolo Solo	... Mr. F. Reilly

—: CHAIRMAN'S ADDRESS.   COLLECTION. :—

❧ PART II. ❧

Pianoforte Solo	... Mr. E. Zardo
Magic	Mr. Charles Thomas Parnell
Song	Miss S. Higgins
Violin Solo	Mr. G. Pierkot
Recitation	Miss F. King
Song	... Miss Egan
Song	... Mr. Reilly

"AMERICA."   "GOD SAVE THE KING."

Accompanist—Miss Irene O'Leary
Committee—Messrs. P. J. Boughal, W. E. Bristol, John K. Nissley
and Charles Thomas Parnell

For a short while after the outbreak of the Great War the two sister ships carried on with a normal service – even with the continuance of that great tradition of the passengers' concert that raised funds for seamen's charities. (Collection of Günter Bäbler)

Gradually the Atlantic service was decreased. The *Mauretania* was laid up in Liverpool, while the *Lusitania* carried on with a reduced service. That is until 7 May 1915, when the *Lusitania*'s homeward journey was fatally terminated by a single torpedo from the Imperial German Navy's U-boat *U-20*. Of the 1,959 people on board, 1,198 were lost including 128 Americans. Public opinion was appalled, as were artists. In England, composer Frank Bridge wrote 'Lament' (dedicated to Catherine, aged 9, *Lusitania* 1915) and Portsmouth marine painter William W. Wyllie produced the graphic image above, 'The Track of *Lusitania*. View of Casualties and Survivors in the Water and in Lifeboats'.

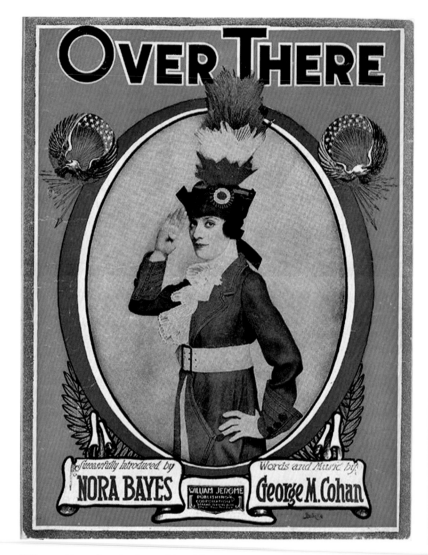

Still smarting after the loss of its citizens who had been on board the *Lusitania* and following subsequent similar events, the United States finally declared war on Germany and her allies on 3 February 1917. It would take another several months for an army to be trained and prepared and it would then take ships like the *Mauretania* to bring the 'Doughboys' over. A popular song at the time had a famous title with an equally popular refrain: 'The Yanks are coming, the Yanks are coming ...!'

A plate, 'All's Well', from *The Look Out*, a book illustrated by Harry Hudson Rodmell showing the *Mauretania* outward-bound from New York and passing the Statue of Liberty.

A few weeks after the tragedy that befell her sister, the *Mauretania* made three trips to the Mediterranean carrying troops destined to fight in the ill-starred Gallipoli campaign, after which she was transformed into a hospital ship to bring the wounded and sick back to Britain, also making three voyages in this guise. As such the liner looked almost her best with a white hull and four buff funnels, rather like the private steam yachts so popular with the ennobled and wealthy.

In 1919 Cunard's express service moved to Southampton and calls into Cherbourg became a feature of the new route. Here Kenneth Shoesmith has evocatively painted the *Mauretania* at Cherbourg at dusk probably after sailing from Southampton that afternoon.

Being the home port of the biggest British liners and a port of call for foreign ships, Southampton was proudly advertised as 'The Gateway to the World'. It was also a base for ship maintenance and repair. In this view the *Mauretania* has just entered – or is about to leave – the flooded Floating Dock for an overhaul, White Star's *Olympic* is at Berth 46 in the Ocean Dock (ex-White Star Dock) and the United States Line's *Leviathan* is at Berth 44. A railway steamer to the Channel Islands (possibly Southern Railways' *Isle of Sark*, *Isle of Guernsey* or *Isle of Jersey*) steams outward-bound in the foreground (right). The shipbuilding yard of John I. Thornycroft can be seen beyond sitting on the far bank of the River Itchen at Woolston. This yard, with a ship repair branch within the docks, would undertake much of the maintenance work on all types of ship.

Right: A well-known and impressive cover to the 1929 Christmas number of the in-house *Cunard* magazine. Although by now the *Mauretania* had surrendered the Blue Ribband to the German liner *Bremen,* she had still distinguished herself by breaking her own record! According to one report, her engines were running 'like sewing machines!' Her previous epithet of 'Queen of the Ocean' was respectfully changed to 'The [Grand] Old Lady of the Atlantic'.

Far right: During the 1920s an annual luxury cruise had been made to the Near East from New York for those with the money to spare. Instead of letting the liner lay more or less idle in New York between crossings during the Great Depression, the *Mauretania* was put on more affordable long-weekend cruises to Bermuda. Later, these cruises would be extended to twelve days with destinations further afield in the Caribbean, her superior speed allowing her to take in many more ports than other ships. In doing so she could impress her cruisers with her legendary speed without the threat of damage otherwise caused by the troublesome North Atlantic.

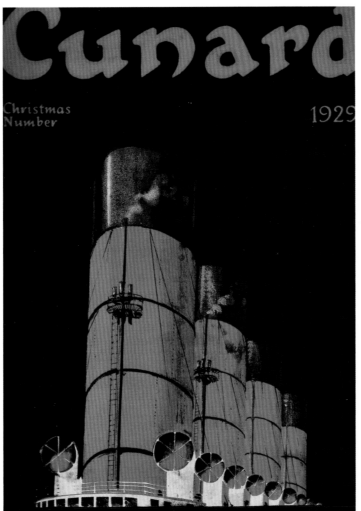

CUNARD'S
FOUR DAY CARE-FREE
WEEK-END
CRUISES
TO
BERMUDA
$50 (UP)

The Cunarder made an occasional cruise to Halifax in Nova Scotia, her Canadian terminus during and after the Great War when gathering or repatriating Canadian troops. In the background can be seen the Nova Scotian Hotel that had been built by Canadian National Railways and opened in June 1930. (Tinted postcard based on a RCAF photograph)

Designed for the weather of the North Atlantic, the great liner did not have air conditioning, only wind scoops fitted to portholes to provide some solace from the heat. This painting, by acclaimed marine artist Stephen Card, shows the liner ('a bloomin' wedding cake') departing New York on a cruise in her new livery. (By kind permission of Stephen Card)

Tempting brochures in best art deco style were issued to lure potential passengers aboard the ship for fun, grand dining, adventure – and (possibly) romance.

One of the favourite entertainments while on board were the well-attended crew's mid-afternoon amateur boxing matches, which attracted a large crowd.

John Jenkins of Portsmouth, one-time bell boy on the *Mauretania*, photographed with a card of congratulation from HM Queen Elizabeth ii to commemorate his 100th birthday. John had joined the *Mauretania* as a 14-year-old and would, in later years after leaving the sea, find employment in Portsmouth's prestigious Royal Dockyard. In June 1944 he was involved with the D-Day landings on Gold Beach as a sergeant in the Royal Pioneer Corps and in later years he was awarded an MBE. At the age of 92 John carried the Olympic torch when it came to his home town and later gave an address to the official gathering in Normandy that marked the seventieth anniversary of the D-Day landings. John passed away one month after his centenary. (By kind permission of Robert Hind)

As in old publicity illustrations, artist Charles Pears has depicted tugs at half-scale to accentuate the stature that 'The Grand Old Lady of the Atlantic' had acquired in the British affection. The *Mauretania* is shown with cut-down masts that enabled her to pass beneath the Forth Rail Bridge (background) en route to her final destination, the shipbreakers at Rosyth. This painting would be hung in the then brand-new Cunarder *Queen Mary* as a tribute, much as HM Queen Elizabeth II would wear a miniature of her father, the late King George VI, on her lapel.

SELECTED BIBLIOGRAPHY

In the creation of this book I resorted to many sources that were cited in my previous publication's bibliography. So, in order to enhance the reader's understanding of the ship, I am repeating some of – and adding to – those books with direct *Mauretania* references and interest. I particularly recommend de Kerbrech and Williams' recent *Harland & Wolff and Workman, Clark: A Golden Age of Shipbuilding in Old Images*, which gives an excellent overview of the heavy industry that was involved in the building of a great ship without the reader having to suffer the danger, noise, heat, cold, grime and long working weeks involved in such a process. Health-and-safety legislation and risk analysis were two concepts that lay in the far and distant future.

BOOKS

Hutchings, David F., *RMS* Mauretania: *Queen of the Ocean* (Cheltenham: The History Press, 2019).
Jordan, Humfrey, Mauretania: *Landfalls and Departures of Twenty-Five Years* (London: Hodder and Stoughton, 1936).
Kerbrech, Richard P. de, *Down Amongst the Black Gang: The World and Workplace of RMS* Titanic's *Stokers* (Cheltenham: The History Press, 2014).
Kerbrech, Richard P. de and Williams, David L., *Harland & Wolff and Workman, Clark: A Golden Age of Shipbuilding in Old Images* (Cheltenham: The History Press, 2021)
Kludas, Arnold, *Record Breakers of the North Atlantic: Blue Riband Liners 1838–1952* (London: Chatham Publishing, 2000).
Layton, J. Kent, *The Unseen* Mauretania *1907: The Ship in Rare Illustrations* (Cheltenham: The History Press, 2021).
Newall, Peter, Mauretania: *Triumph and Resurrection* (London: Ships in Focus Publications, 2006).
Smith, Ken, *Pride of the Tyne* (Newcastle: Newcastle Libraries & Information Department and Tyne & Wear Museums, 1997).
Warren, Mark D., *The Cunard Turbine-Driven Quadruple-Screw Atlantic Liner* Mauretania (Wellingborough: Patrick Stephens, 1987).

ARTICLES AND PAPERS

Buxton, Ian (Professor), '*Mauretania* and Her Builders', *The Mariner's Mirror*, Vol. 82 No. 1, 1986, pp.55–73.
Lloyd's Calendar, 1958, Lloyd's London, England.
Mauretania, Engineering, Special Edition, 8 November 1907.
Wilkinson, M., 'The Demolition of the *Mauretania*' (Manchester Association of Engineers, read on 15 March 1940 – Session 1939–40).

Progress Tests

Spelling

Louis Fidge

Hachette UK's policy is to use papers that are natural, renewable and recyclable products and made from wood grown in sustainable forests. The logging and manufacturing processes are expected to conform to the environmental regulations of the country of origin.

Orders: please contact Bookpoint Ltd, 130 Milton Park, Abingdon, Oxon OX14 4SB. Telephone: (44) 01235 827720. Fax: (44) 01235 400454. Lines are open 9.00a.m.–5.00p.m., Monday to Saturday, with a 24-hour message answering service. Visit our website at www.hoddereducation.co.uk.

© Louis Fidge 2013
First published in 2007 exclusively for WHSmith by
Hodder Education
An Hachette UK Company
338 Euston Road
London NW1 3BH

This second edition first published in 2013 exclusively for WHSmith by Hodder Education.

Impression number   10 9 8 7 6 5 4 3 2 1
Year   2018 2017 2016 2015 2014 2013

Cover illustration by Oxford Designers and Illustrators Ltd
All other illustrations by Fakenham Prepress Solutions, Fakenham, Norfolk NR21 8NN
Typeset in 16pt Folio by Fakenham Prepress Solutions, Fakenham, Norfolk NR21 8NN
Printed in Great Britain by Hobbs the Printers Ltd, Totton, Hampshire SO40 3WX

A catalogue record for this title is available from the British Library.

ISBN: 978 1444 188 950

**Age 10–11
Year 6
Key Stage 2**

Introduction

Progress Tests: Spelling

- Spelling is a key feature of the National Curriculum and the National Literacy Framework.
- Children need to be able to spell in order to read and write fluently and confidently.
- Good spelling is essential in all areas of the curriculum.
- Learning to spell requires constant practice and reinforcement.
- This series of 'teach and test' books will help build your child's confidence and ability in spelling.

Features of the books

- Each test:
  - has a clear spelling focus
  - introduces ten words which contain the same spelling focus
  - has a range of activities which help your child to learn to spell the words
  - finishes with a spelling test, using the ten Test words.
- Answers to the activities may be found on pages 34–40.
- A record sheet is provided on page 3 on which your child can keep a record of all spelling test scores.

How to do the tests

- Do one test each week.
- Agree on a set time with your child, and keep it the same each week if possible.
- Ensure your child can read the Test words at the top of the page and knows their meanings.
- Encourage your child to do the activities to help learn the words.
- On completion of the activities, get your child to do the spelling test.

How to do the spelling tests

- Turn to pages 41–48 and find the appropriate answer sheet to complete.
- Ask your child to look back at the Test words in the unit and study these again for a short while.
- Then either:
  - copy out the words and read them slowly to your child (or get another adult or child to read them)

  or:
  - ask your child to write the words from memory (without copying them!).
- When the spelling test has been completed, ask your child to mark it by referring back to the Test words and checking their spellings.
- After each spelling test, ask your child to colour in the score on the record sheet on the inside back cover.

Test 1: Revision (1) the suffixes -able and -ible

Test words

comfortable suitable miserable valuable fashionable
possible horrible sensible flexible incredible

1 Read the ten Test words.

2 Complete each word with **-able** or **-ible**.

a) comfort_____   b) incred_____

c) fashion_____   d) poss_____

e) horr_____   f) suit_____

g) flex_____   h) miser_____

i) valu_____   j) sens_____

3 Use the correct word in each sentence.

a) The monster pulled a _____ face.

b) The jewellery was very _____.

c) I buy new clothes because I like to look _____.

d) The film was not _____ for children.

e) The damp weather made me feel _____.

f) Is it _____ to fly to Mars?

g) When you can bend something you say it is _____.

h) Something almost unbelievable is said to be _____.

i) It is _____ not to run across a busy road.

j) The armchair was very _____.

4 Now do **Spelling Test 1** on page 41.

Test 2: Revision (2) the suffix -ment

Test words

> agreement amusement entertainment arrangement employment
> advertisement involvement government improvement astonishment

1. Read the ten Test words.

2. Write the noun that can be made from each verb.

   a) agree   *agreement*   **b)** involve   _____

   c) arrange   _____   **d)** govern   _____

   e) improve   _____   **f)** astonish   _____

   g) amuse   _____   **h)** entertain   _____

   i) employ   _____   **j)** advertise   _____

3. Use the correct word in each sentence.

   a) The man laughed with _____ at the clown.

   b) We made an _____ not to argue any more.

   c) The _____ was trying to sell a car.

   d) The _____ made a new law.

   e) To my _____ I won first prize.

   f) He has been looking for _____ as a teacher.

   g) I must make an _____ in my handwriting.

   h) The _____ of items in the shop window was dull.

   i) The man had no _____ with the gang of thieves.

   j) The _____ on TV was exciting.

4. Now do **Spelling Test 2** on page 41.

Test 3: Revision (3) the suffixes -tion and -sion

Test words

operation education examination conversation information
explosion decision division invasion inclusion

1 Read the ten Test words.

2 Complete each word with **tion** or **sion**.

a) informa*tion*

b) inclu_____

c) inva_____

d) conversa_____

e) examina_____

f) divi_____

g) deci_____

h) educa_____

i) opera_____

j) explo_____

3 Use the correct word in each sentence.

a) When the bomb blew up there was a loud _____.

b) I think _____ sums are quite hard.

c) The general planned an _____ of the country.

d) It was a difficult _____ to know what to do.

e) The group's _____ of Sam made him very happy.

f) The doctor performed the _____ in hospital.

g) You go to school to get an _____.

h) I went to the library to get some _____ about dinosaurs.

i) The two men had a long _____ about sport.

j) The pupils took the important _____ at school.

4 Now do **Spelling Test 3** on page 41.

Test 4: Revision (4) **wa** and **qua** words

Test words

watch	wash	wander	wallet	swamp
quality	quantity	squat	squash	squabble

1 Read the ten Test words.

2 Write the word that means:

a) like a purse _____

b) to walk slowly _____

c) tells you the time _____

d) to clean with water _____

e) to argue _____

f) to make flat _____

g) very wet ground _____

h) to bend down _____

i) how good or bad something is _____

j) an amount of something _____

3 Use the correct word in each sentence.

a) A _____ tells you the time.

b) The two children had a _____ over a toy.

c) I love to _____ quietly through the woods.

d) The man lost his _____ containing all his money.

e) When you get dirty you have to _____.

f) I had to _____ down to look under the table.

g) If you squeeze an empty can you can _____ it.

h) The material of the dress was a good _____.

i) Don't go in the _____ because alligators live there!

j) A gross is a large _____.

4 Now do **Spelling Test 4** on page 41.

6

Test 5: Words in which **o** sounds like **u**

● Test words

> sponge   front   discover   worry   wonderful
> money   nothing   month   glove   oven

1 Read the ten Test words.

2 Write the words with:

    a) four letters _____

    b) five letters _____ _____

    _____ _____ _____

    c) six letters _____

    d) seven letters _____

    e) eight letters _____

    f) nine letters _____

3 Use the correct word in each sentence.

    a) You cook things in an _____.

    b) To _____ means to find out.

    c) You wear a _____ on your hand.

    d) When you _____ you are afraid something bad will happen.

    e) March is the _____ after February.

    f) The opposite of 'back' is _____.

    g) A _____ soaks up water.

    h) You spend _____ in a shop.

    i) The opposite of 'something' is _____.

    j) I had a _____ time at the party.

4 Now do **Spelling Test 5** on page 42.

Test 6: Syllables

Test words

expensive marvellous punishment establish wonderful
hospital underground singular attention advertise

1 Read the ten Test words.

2 Fill in the missing syllable and then write the whole word.

a) mar+vel+*lous* = _marvellous_

b) won+_____+ful = _____

c) at+ten+_____ = _____

d) _____+der+ground = _____

e) _____+pen+sive = _____

f) es+tab+_____ = _____

g) ad+ver+_____ = _____

h) _____+ish+ment = _____

i) _____+pit+al = _____

j) sin+_____+lar = _____

3 Use the correct word in each sentence.

a) The ambulance took Ben to the _____.

b) Worms live _____.

c) You might _____ something if you wanted to sell it.

d) _____ means just one thing.

e) The teacher had to shout to gain the children's _____.

f) The _____ dress cost a lot of money.

4 Now do **Spelling Test 6** on page 42.

Test 7: Unstressed vowels

Test words

vegetable chocolate mathematics secretary history diamond poisonous freedom separate interesting

1. Read the ten Test words above. The letters in **bold** are unstressed vowels. When we say these words we don't always pronounce the vowels clearly.

2. Write the words with:

   a) an unstressed **a** _____ _____ _____

   b) an unstressed **e** _____ _____ _____

   c) an unstressed **o** _____ _____

   _____ _____

3. Use the correct word in each sentence.

   a) The study of numbers is called _____.

   b) The prisoner made a dash for _____.

   c) In _____ we study the past.

   d) Something _____ is not joined to anything.

   e) A potato is a type of _____.

   f) I am reading an _____ book.

   g) I ate a bar of _____.

   h) The _____ answered the telephone.

   i) Some snakes are _____.

   j) A _____ is a very hard stone.

4. Now do **Spelling Test 7** on page 42.

Test words

__expensive __accurate __sane __visible __complete
__possible __perfect __pure __patient __practical

1 Add **in-** to the top five words above.
Add **im-** to the bottom five words above.
Read the ten Test words you make.

2 Choose **in-** or **im-** to complete each word.

a) ____perfect **b)** ____sane **c)** ____practical

d) ____visible **e)** ____expensive **f)** ____pure

g) ____possible **h)** ____complete **i)** ____accurate

j) ____patient

3 Write the **in-** words in alphabetical order.

_____ _____ _____

_____ _____

4 Write the **im-** words in alphabetical order.

_____ _____ _____

_____ _____

5 Now do **Spelling Test 8** on page 42.

Test 9: Prefixes and meanings

Test words

subway surplus circumference telephone autograph
submarine circumstances autobiography surface television

 1 Read the ten Test words above.

2 Write the words which begin with:

   a) **sub-** ('under')   _____ _____

   b) **sur-** ('above')   _____ _____

   c) **circum-** ('around') _____ _____

   d) **tele-** ('from afar') _____ _____

   e) **auto-** ('self')   _____ _____

3 Write the word that means:

   a) a boat that goes under the sea   _____

   b) a path underground   _____

   c) it receives pictures from a distance   _____

   d) you use it to speak to people from afar   _____

   e) the story of a person's life written
       by themselves   _____

   f) a person's own signature   _____

   g) the distance around a circle   _____

   h) the conditions surrounding an event   _____

   i) the outside of something   _____

   j) the amount left over   _____

4 Now do **Spelling Test 9** on page 43.

Test 10: The suffixes **-ant** and **-ent**

● Test words

arrog____	abund____	extravag____	ignor____	fragr____
obedi____	intellig____	magnific____	viol____	evid____

1 Add **-ant** to the end of the top five words above.
Add **-ent** to the end of the bottom five words above.
Read the ten Test words you make.

2 Write the words that begin with:

a) a _____ _____   b) e _____ _____

c) i _____ _____   d) f _____

e) m _____   f) o _____

g) v _____

3 Write the words that contain:

a) ag _____ _____ _____

b) ig _____ _____

c) og _____   d) ol _____

e) vid _____   f) bun _____

g) bed _____

4 Now do **Spelling Test 10** on page 43.

12

Test 11: The suffixes -ary, -ery and -ory

Test words

pottery   library   bakery   factory   nursery
estuary   laboratory   dormitory   granary   brewery

1 Read the ten Test words above.

2 Complete the chart.

-ary words	-ery words	-ory words

3 Write the name of the place where:

a) pots are made _____   **b)** scientists work _____

c) books are kept _____   **d)** beer is made _____

e) a river meets the sea _____

f) bread is made _____   **g)** grain is stored _____

h) young children go to school _____

i) there are lots of beds _____

j) manufacturing takes place _____

4 Now do **Spelling Test 11** on page 43.

13

Test 12: Number prefixes

triangle	unicorn	trio	bisect	unit
bicycle	unique	bilingual	tripod	uniform

1 Read the ten Test words above.

2 Complete the chart.

uni- words	**bi-** words	**tri-** words

3 Write the word that means:

a) the only one of its kind _____

b) all the same _____

c) one of something _____

d) a magical horse with a horn _____

e) to cut in two _____

f) speaks two languages _____

g) a vehicle with two wheels _____

h) a shape with three sides _____

i) a stand with three legs _____

j) a group of three _____

4 Now do **Spelling Test 12** on page 43.

Test 13: Common letter strings (1)

Test words

tongue   musician   harbour   engineer   surprise
advertise   volunteer   catalogue   vapour   librarian

1. Read the ten Test words.

2. Write the words containing the following letter strings:

   a) ue   *tongue*   *catalogue*

   b) ian   _____   _____

   c) ise   _____   _____

   d) our   _____   _____

   e) eer   _____   _____

3. Use the correct word in each sentence.

   a) It is rude to stick your _____ out at anyone.

   b) If we want to sell anything we _____ it.

   c) An _____ makes and repairs engines.

   d) The ship sheltered in the _____ during the storm

   e) _____ is steam, mist or smoke floating in the air.

   f) It was a lovely _____ to receive a present.

   g) I looked in the _____ to find the toy I wanted.

   h) The _____ played the trombone.

   i) If you _____, you offer to do something.

   j) The _____ found the book I wanted in the library.

4. Now do **Spelling Test 13** on page 44.

Test 14: Common letter strings (2)

Test words

alarm	daughter	drought	flood	gather
rather	swarm	stood	laughter	thought

1 Read the ten Test words.

2 Write the pairs of words with the same letter strings.

a) alarm   *swarm*   **b)** daughter   _____

c) drought   _____   **d)** flood   _____

e) gather   _____

3 Use the correct word in each sentence.

a) The _____ of bees flew away from their hive.

b) After all the rain there was a terrible _____.

c) Last night I _____ I heard a noise downstairs.

d) There was a lot of fun and _____ at the party.

e) The burglar _____ went off when the thief broke into the house.

f) I would _____ have an ice cream than a lolly.

g) The small child _____ on tiptoe to reach the top shelf.

h) Anna is Mrs Barton's _____.

i) In the autumn I like to _____ pine cones from the wood.

j) We had no rain for months so there was a bad _____.

4 Now do **Spelling Test 14** on page 44.

Test 15: Rhyming letter strings

● Test words

spoil	daughter	eight	heard	bruise
shoes	wait	royal	absurd	water

1 Read the ten Test words.

2 Write the word that rhymes with:

a) eight _____ **b)** bruise _____

c) royal _____ **d)** heard _____

e) water _____

3 Use the correct word in each sentence.

a) A drink of _____ quenches your thirst.

b) The prince was a member of the _____ family.

c) The mother bought her _____ a new dress.

d) I got a big purple _____ where I bumped my arm.

e) It is _____ to say the sun is green.

f) I tried hard not to _____ my work by rushing it.

g) There were _____ people in the bus queue.

h) My new _____ were uncomfortable when I first wore them.

i) I had to _____ ten minutes for the shop to open.

j) Have you ever _____ of the Abominable Snowman?

4 Now do **Spelling Test 15** on page 44.

Test 16: Spelling rule (1)

● Test words

th____f p____ce bel____ve w____ld misch____f
n____ce ach____ve br____f gr____ve sh____ld

1 Add **ie** to the words above. Remember the rule:
Put **i** (when it sounds like **ee**) before **e** except after **c**.

2 Write the words containing these letter patterns.

a) ief _____ _____ _____

b) iece _____ _____

c) ieve _____ _____ _____

d) ield _____ _____

3 Change some letters. Read the new words you make.

a) Change the **th** in **th**ief to **br**   *brief*

b) Change the **br** in **br**ief to **misch**   _____

c) Change the **misch** in **misch**ief to **th**   _____

d) Change the **p** in **p**iece to **n**   _____

e) Change the **gr** in **gr**ieve to **bel**   _____

f) Change the **bel** in **bel**ieve to **ach**   _____

g) Change the **ach** in **ach**ieve to **gr**   _____

h) Change the **w** in **w**ield to **sh**   _____

i) Change the **sh** in **sh**ield to **w**   _____

j) Change the **n** in **n**iece to **p**   _____

4 Now do **Spelling Test 16** on page 44.

18

Test 17: Spelling rule (2)

Test words

> excitable   freezer   refusal   famous   relative
> reversible   deserving   finest   shaken   retired

1 Read the ten Test words above.

2 Remember the rule:
When a word ends with a **consonant + e**, we usually drop the **e** before adding a suffix that begins with a vowel.

3 Write the words that are built from:

a) fame _____ **b)** shake _____

c) freeze _____ **d)** excite _____

e) fine _____ **f)** retire _____

g) reverse _____ **h)** relate _____

i) deserve _____ **j)** refuse _____

4 Do the word sums. Spell the words correctly!

a) relate+ive = _____ **b)** fine+est = _____

c) retire+ed = _____ **d)** freeze+er = _____

e) fame+ous = _____ **f)** shake+en = _____

g) excite+able = _____ **h)** refuse+al = _____

i) reverse+ible = _____ **j)** deserve+ing = _____

5 Now do **Spelling Test 17** on page 45.

Test words

notice_____   replace_____   change_____   manage_____   charge_____

courage_____   outrage_____   advantage_____   disadvantage_____   gorge_____

1 Add **-able** to the end of the top five words above.
Add **-ous** to the end of the bottom five words above.
Read the ten Test words you make.

2 Remember the rule:
When adding a suffix beginning with **a** or **o** after a word ending with **ce** or **ge**, we keep the **e** to keep the **c** and **g** 'soft'.

3 Write the word that means:

a) can be changed _____

b) can be managed _____

c) can be noticed _____

d) can be charged _____

e) can be replaced _____

f) lovely to look at _____

g) to your advantage _____

h) very brave _____

i) very unusual _____

j) opposite of advantageous _____

4 Now do **Spelling Test 18** on page 45.

Test 19: Spelling rule (4)

⬤ Test words

> rebelled regretting traveller signaller permitting
> quarrelling admitted deterred beginner occurred

1 Read the ten Test words above.

2 Remember the rule:
In words of more than one syllable, if the last syllable ends with a single vowel and a consonant, we double the consonant before we add a suffix beginning with a vowel.

3 Do the word sums. Spell the words correctly!

    a) rebel+ed = _____   **b)** occur+ed = _____

    c) admit+ed = _____   **d)** deter+ed = _____

    e) regret+ing = _____   **f)** quarrel+ing = _____

    f) permit+ing = _____   **h)** travel+er = _____

    i) begin+er = _____   **j)** signal+er _____

4 Write the words ending with:

    a) ing _____ _____ _____

    b) ed _____ _____ _____ _____

    c) er _____ _____ _____

5 Now do **Spelling Test 19** on page 45.

Test 20: Homophones

Test words

steal	berth	muscles	waste	pray
mussels	prey	waist	steel	birth

1 Read the ten Test words above.

2 Write the word that sounds like:

a) steel _____

b) berth _____

c) muscles _____

d) waist _____

e) pray _____

3 Write the word that means:

a) a type of metal _____

b) to say prayers _____

c) where ships dock _____

d) shellfish _____

e) hunted animals _____

f) being born _____

g) to take what is not yours _____

h) to use up carelessly _____

i) they help you move your body _____

j) part of your body below your ribs _____

4 Now do **Spelling Test 20** on page 45.

Test 21: Word endings -ate and -ite

Test words

priv_____ decor_____ consider_____ deliber_____ certific_____
defin_____ appet_____ exquis_____ dynam_____ oppos_____

1) Add **-ate** to the top five words above.
Add **-ite** to the bottom five words above.
Read the ten Test words you make.

2) Write the words with:

a) two syllables _____

b) three syllables _____ _____ _____

_____ _____ _____

c) four syllables _____ _____ _____

3) Write the **-ate** words in alphabetical order.

_____ _____ _____

_____ _____

4) Write the **-ite** words in alphabetical order.

_____ _____ _____

_____ _____

5) Now do **Spelling Test 21** on page 46.

23

Test 22: Words within words

Test words

island   separate   business   breadth   conscience
country   government   sword   mosquito   cupboard

1   Read the ten Test words in the box above.

2   Write the words with:

a)   five letters   _____

b)   six letters   _____

c)   seven letters   _____ _____

d)   eight letters   _____ _____

_____ _____

e)   ten letters   _____ _____

3   Write the word that contains:

a)   count   _____   **b)**   rate   _____

c)   bread   _____   **d)**   cup   _____

e)   land   _____   **f)**   govern   _____

g)   bus   _____   **h)**   science   _____

i)   word   _____   **j)**   quit   _____

4   Now do **Spelling Test 22** on page 46.

Test 23: Unusual plurals

Test words

mice	geese	women	gateaux	cacti
sheep	salmon	aircraft	deer	trout

1 Read the ten Test words above. They are all plural nouns.

2 Write the plural form of each singular noun below.

a) goose _____

b) woman _____

c) cactus _____

d) mouse _____

e) gateau _____

f) aircraft _____

g) deer _____

h) salmon _____

i) sheep _____

j) trout _____

3 Write the nouns whose singular and plural forms are spelt the same.

_____ _____ _____ _____ _____

4 Write the correct plural form of each noun in brackets in these sentences.

a) There were lots of _____ (mouse) in the house.

b) The two _____ (woman) went to the shop.

c) The _____ (cactus) were very prickly.

d) The farmer had several _____ (goose).

e) We bought three chocolate _____ (gateau).

5 Now do **Spelling Test 23** on page 46.

Test 24: **ci** and **ti**

● Test words

> spe____al   an____ent   deli____ous   artifi____al   effi____ent
> pa____ent   cau____ous   ini____al   infec____ous   ambi____ous

1 Fill in the missing **ci** in the top five words above.
Fill in the missing **ti** in the bottom five words above.
Read the ten Test words you make.

2 Write the words that end with:

a) al   _____ _____ _____

b) ent   _____ _____ _____

c) ous   _____ _____ _____ _____

3 Use a dictionary if necessary and write the word that means:

a) willing to wait without complaining   _____

b) very old   _____

c) tasting very nice   _____

d) first   _____

e) not real   _____

f) spreading disease   _____

g) neat and skilful   _____

h) wanting to be successful   _____

i) slow and careful   _____

j) out of the ordinary   _____

4 Now do **Spelling Test 24** on page 46.

Test 25: Word origins – Latin

Test words

> signature applaud video audience spectator
> scribble edible computer annual proverb

1 Read the ten Test words which all come from Latin.

2 Add the missing final syllable in each word.

a) sig/na/_____   **b)** ap/_____

c) vid/e/_____   **d)** au/di/_____

e) spec/ta/_____   **f)** scrib/_____

g) e/dib/_____   **h)** com/pu/_____

i) an/nu/_____   **j)** pro/_____

3 Complete the chart.

Latin word	Meaning	Test word
videre	to see	*video*
edere	to eat	
audire	to hear	
laudare	to praise	
scribere	to write	
spectare	to watch	
putare	to think	
signum	sign	
verbum	word	
annus	year	

4 Now do **Spelling Test 25** on page 47.

Test 26: Word origins – Greek

● Test words

> politics   astrology   biology   telephone   telescope
> autograph   grammar   sphere   optician   melody

1 Read the ten Test words above. They all originate from Ancient Greek.

2 Write the ten words in alphabetical order.

_____ _____ _____ _____ _____

_____ _____ _____ _____ _____

3 Complete the chart.

Greek word	Meaning	Test word
bios	life	*biology*
phone	sound	
optikus	to do with sight	
aster	star	
grapho	I write	
gramma	the written word	
skopeo	I see	
oide	a song	
sphaira	globe	
polis	city	

4 Now do **Spelling Test 26** on page 47.

Test 27: Word origins – Anglo-Saxon

Test words

wisdom	barrow	fleet	wagon	engrave
weigh	witness	groove	afloat	burden

1. Read the ten Test words above. They all originate from Anglo-Saxon (old English).

2. Write the words containing:

   a) five letters _____ _____ _____

   b) six letters _____ _____ _____

   _____ _____

   c) seven letters _____ _____

3. Complete the chart.

Anglo-Saxon word	Meaning	pair of Test words
witan	to know	*wisdom witness*
floetan	to float	
grafan	to dig	
beran	to carry	
wegan	to move	

4. Now do **Spelling Test 27** on page 47.

Test 28: Key words (1)

● Test words

> recommend parallel address disappear assistant
> professor successful opportunity necessary beginning

1 Read the ten Test words. They all contain tricky double letters!

2 Write the words that contain:

a) mm _____   **b)** nn _____

c) ll _____   **d)** pp _____ _____

e) ss _____ _____ _____

_____ _____

3 Write the word that means:

a) two lines the same distance apart _____

b) a person who teaches in a university _____

c) to go out of sight _____

d) starting _____

e) someone who helps _____

f) where you live _____

g) turning out well _____

h) needed _____

i) to praise or speak well of _____

j) a chance to do something _____

4 Now do **Spelling Test 28** on page 47.

Test 29: Key words (2)

 Test words

| embarrass exaggerate accompany abbreviate possession |
| immediate disappoint tomorrow drizzle accommodate |

1 Read the ten Test words. They all contain tricky double letters!

2 Write the top five words in alphabetical order.

_____ _____ _____ _____ _____

3 Write the bottom five words in alphabetical order.

_____ _____ _____ _____ _____

4 Write the word that means:

a) straight away _____

b) the day after today _____

c) to make room for _____

d) something that belongs to you _____

e) to shorten _____

f) a light rain _____

g) to fall short of your expectations _____

h) to make someone feel awkward _____

i) to make something seem better than it really is _____

j) to go with someone _____

5 Now do **Spelling Test 29** on page 48.

Test 30: Key words (3)

Test words

florist   chauffeur   mechanic   sculptor   joiner
ventriloquist   architect   optician   electrician   pianist

1   Read the ten Test words.

2   **a)**   Write the top five Test words in alphabetical order.

   _____   _____   _____   _____   _____

   b)   Write the bottom five Test words in alphabetical order.

   _____   _____   _____   _____   _____

3   Write the word that means someone who:

   a)   plans new buildings   _____

   b)   is paid to drive a car   _____

   c)   repairs many kinds of electrical things   _____

   d)   sells flowers and plants   _____

   e)   makes things out of wood   _____

   f)   repairs machines and engines   _____

   g)   looks after people's eyes   _____

   h)   plays the piano   _____

   i)   carves statues or shapes from stone   _____

   j)   seems to be able to make a puppet speak   _____

4   Now do **Spelling Test 30** on page 48.

Test words

antique	sandwich	library	mathematics	parallel
receipt	debt	restaurant	soldier	weight

1 Read the ten Test Words. These words are quite tricky to spell!

2 Fill in the missing letters and then write the whole word.

a) antiq *u e*   *antique*   **b)** san__wich   _____

c) lib__ary   _____   **d)** math__matics   _____

e) para__el   _____   **f)** rec__t   _____

g) de__t   _____   **h)** rest__rant   _____

i) sol_____   _____   **j)** w_____   _____

3 Write the word that means:

a) a member of the army   _____

b) the amount of money you owe   _____

c) how heavy something is   _____

d) linesthat are always the same distance apart   _____

e) a place where books are stored   _____

f) something that is old and valuable   _____

g) two slices of bread with a filling   _____

h) the study of numbers   _____

i) a note recording what you have been given   _____

j) a place where you can eat   _____

4 Now do **Spelling Test 31** on page 48.

Answers

Test 1

2 a comfortable b incredible
  c fashionable d possible
  e horrible f suitable
  g flexible h miserable
  i valuable j sensible
3 a horrible b valuable
  c fashionable d suitable
  e miserable f possible
  g flexible h incredible
  i sensible j comfortable

Test 2

2 a agreement b involvement
  c arrangement d government
  e improvement f astonishment
  g amusement h entertainment
  i employment j advertisement
3 a amusement b agreement
  c advertisement d government
  e astonishment f employment
  g improvement h arrangement
  i involvement j entertainment

Test 3

2 a information b inclusion
  c invasion d conversation
  e examination f division
  g decision h education
  i operation j explosion

3 a explosion b division
  c invasion d decision
  e inclusion f operation
  g education h information
  i conversation j examination

Test 4

2 a wallet b wander
  c watch d wash
  e squabble f squash
  g swamp h squat
  i quality j quantity
3 a watch b squabble
  c wander d wallet
  e wash f squat
  g squash h quality
  i swamp j quantity

Test 5

2 a oven
  b front worry money month glove
  c sponge
  d nothing
  e discover
  f wonderful
3 a oven b discover c glove
  d worry e month f front
  g sponge h money i nothing
  j wonderful

Test 6

2 a marvellous   b wonderful
   c attention   d underground
   e expensive   f establish
   g advertise   h punishment
   i hospital   j singular
3 a hospital   b underground
   c advertise   d Singular
   e attention   f expensive

Test 7

2 a secretary diamond separate
   b vegetable mathematics
     interesting
   c chocolate history poisonous
     freedom
3 a mathematics   b freedom
   c history   d separate
   e vegetable   f interesting
   g chocolate   h secretary
   i poisonous   j diamond

Test 8

1 inexpensive inaccurate insane
   invisible incomplete impossible
   imperfect impure impatient
   impractical
2 a imperfect   b insane
   c impractical   d invisible
   e inexpensive   f impure
   g impossible   h incomplete
   i inaccurate   j impatient
3 inaccurate incomplete
   inexpensive insane invisible
4 impatient imperfect impossible
   impractical impure

Test 9

2 a subway   submarine
   b surplus   surface
   c circumference   circumstances
   d telephone   television
   e autograph   autobiography
3 a submarine   b subway
   c television   d telephone
   e autobiography f autograph
   g circumference
   h circumstances
   i surface   j surplus

Test 10

1 arrogant abundant extravagant
   ignorant fragrant obedient
   intelligent magnificent violent
   evident
2 a arrogant   abundant
   b extravagant   evident
   c ignorant   intelligent
   d fragrant   e magnificent
   f obedient   g violent
3 a extravagant fragrant magnificent
   b ignorant intelligent
   c arrogant   d violent
   e evident   f abundant
   g obedient

Test 11

2 **-ary** words: library estuary granary
-ery words: pottery bakery
nursery brewery
-ory words: factory laboratory
dormitory

3 a pottery b laboratory
c library d brewery
e estuary f bakery
g granary h nursery
i dormitory j factory

Test 12

2 **uni-** words: unicorn unit unique
uniform
bi- words: bisect bicycle bilingual
tri- words: triangle trio tripod

3 a unique b uniform c unit
d unicorn e bisect f bilingual
g bicycle h triangle i tripod
j trio

Test 13

2 a tongue catalogue
b musician librarian
c advertise surprise
d vapour harbour
e engineer volunteer

3 a tongue b advertise
c engineer d harbour
e Vapour f surprise
g catalogue h musician
i volunteer j librarian

Test 14

2 a swarm b laughter c thought
d stood e rather

3 a swarm b flood c thought
d laughter e alarm f rather
g stood h daughter i gather
j drought

Test 15

2 a wait b shoes c spoil
d absurd e daughter

3 a water b royal c daughter
d bruise e absurd f spoil
g eight h shoes i wait
j heard

Test 16

1 thief piece believe wield
   mischief niece achieve brief
   grieve shield
2 a thief mischief brief
   b piece niece
   c believe achieve grieve
   d wield shield
3 a brief   b mischief c thief
   d niece   e believe   f achieve
   g grieve   h shield   i wield
   j piece

Test 17

3 a famous   b shaken
   c freezer   d excitable
   e finest   f retired
   g reversible   h relative
   i deserving   j refusal
4 a relative   b finest
   c retired   d freezer
   e famous   f shaken
   g excitable   h refusal
   i reversible   j deserving

Test 18

1 noticeable replaceable
   changeable manageable
   chargeable courageous
   outrageous advantageous
   disadvantageous gorgeous

2 a changeable   b manageable
   c noticeable   d chargeable
   e replaceable   f gorgeous
   g advantageous h courageous
   i outrageous   j disadvantageous

Test 19

2 a rebelled   b occurred
   c admitted   d deterred
   e regretting   f quarrelling
   g permitting   h traveller
   i beginner   j signaller
3 a regretting permitting quarrelling
   b rebelled admitted deterred
      occurred
   c traveller signaller beginner

Test 20

2 a steal   b birth
   c mussels   d waste
   e prey
3 a steel   b pray
   c berth   d mussels
   e prey   f birth
   g steal   h waste
   i muscles   j waist

Test 21

1 private decorate considerate deliberate certificate
  definite appetite exquisite dynamite opposite

2 a private
  b decorate definite appetite exquisite dynamite opposite
  c considerate deliberate certificate

3 certificate considerate decorate deliberate private

4 appetite definite dynamite exquisite opposite

Test 22

2 a sword   b island
  c country breadth
  d separate business mosquito cupboard
  e conscience government

3 a country   b separate
  c breadth   d cupboard
  e island   f government
  g business   h conscience
  i sword   j mosquito

Test 23

2 a geese   b women   c cacti
  d mice   e gateaux f aircraft
  g deer   h salmon   i sheep
  j trout

3 sheep salmon aircraft deer trout

4 a mice   b women   c cacti
  d geese   e gateaux

Test 24

1 special ancient delicious artificial efficient
  patient cautious initial infectious ambitious

2 a special artificial initial
  b ancient efficient patient
  c delicious cautious infectious ambitious

3 a patient   b ancient
  c delicious   d initial
  e artificial   f infectious
  g efficient   h ambitious
  i cautious   j special

Test 25

2 a sig/na/ture   b ap/plaud
  c vid/e/o   d au/di/ence
  e spec/ta/tor   f scrib/ble
  g e/dib/le   h com/pu/ter
  i an/nu/al   j pro/verb

3 videre – video; edere – edible; audire – audience; laudare – applaud; scribere – scribble; spectare – spectator; putare – computer; signum – signature; verbum – proverb; annus – annual

Test 26

2 astrology autograph biology grammar melody optician politics sphere telephone telescope

3 bios – biology; phone – telephone; optikus – optician; aster – astrology; grapho – autograph; gramma – grammar; skopeo – telescope; oide – melody; sphaira – sphere; polis – politics

Test 27

2 a fleet wagon weigh
  b wisdom barrow groove afloat burden
  c engrave witness

4 witan – wisdom witness; floetan – fleet afloat; grafan – engrave groove; beran – barrow burden; wegan – wagon weigh

Test 28

2 a recommend
  b beginning
  c parallel
  d disappear opportunity
  e address assistant professor successful necessary

3 a parallel   b professor
  c disappear   d beginning
  e assistant   f address
  g successful   h necessary
  i recommend   j opportunity

Test 29

2 abbreviate accompany embarrass exaggerate possession

3 accommodate disappoint drizzle immediate tomorrow

4 a immediate   b tomorrow
  c accommodate d possession
  e abbreviate   f drizzle
  g disappoint   h embarrass
  i exaggerate   j accompany

Test 30

2 a chauffeur florist joiner mechanic sculptor
  b architect electrician optician pianist ventriloquist

3 a architect   b chauffeur
  c electrician   d florist
  e joiner   f mechanic
  g optician   h pianist
  i sculptor   j ventriloquist

Test 31

2 a antique   b sandwich
   c library   d mathematics
   e parallel   f receipt
   g debt   h restaurant
   i soldier   j weight

3 a soldier   b debt
   c weight   d parallel
   e library   f antique
   g sandwich   h mathematics
   i receipt   j restaurant

Spelling test answers

Test 1

1 _____
2 _____
3 _____
4 _____
5 _____
6 _____
7 _____
8 _____
9 _____
10 _____

Score ____

Test 2

1 _____
2 _____
3 _____
4 _____
5 _____
6 _____
7 _____
8 _____
9 _____
10 _____

Score ____

Test 3

1 _____
2 _____
3 _____
4 _____
5 _____
6 _____
7 _____
8 _____
9 _____
10 _____

Score ____

Test 4

1 _____
2 _____
3 _____
4 _____
5 _____
6 _____
7 _____
8 _____
9 _____
10 _____

Score ____

Test 5

1 _____
2 _____
3 _____
4 _____
5 _____
6 _____
7 _____
8 _____
9 _____
10 _____

Score ____

Test 6

1 _____
2 _____
3 _____
4 _____
5 _____
6 _____
7 _____
8 _____
9 _____
10 _____

Score ____

Test 7

1 _____
2 _____
3 _____
4 _____
5 _____
6 _____
7 _____
8 _____
9 _____
10 _____

Score ____

Test 8

1 _____
2 _____
3 _____
4 _____
5 _____
6 _____
7 _____
8 _____
9 _____
10 _____

Score ____

Test 9

1 _____

2 _____

3 _____

4 _____

5 _____

6 _____

7 _____

8 _____

9 _____

10 _____

Score ____

Test 10

1 _____

2 _____

3 _____

4 _____

5 _____

6 _____

7 _____

8 _____

9 _____

10 _____

Score ____

Test 11

1 _____

2 _____

3 _____

4 _____

5 _____

6 _____

7 _____

8 _____

9 _____

10 _____

Score ____

Test 12

1 _____

2 _____

3 _____

4 _____

5 _____

6 _____

7 _____

8 _____

9 _____

10 _____

Score ____

Test 13

1 _____
2 _____
3 _____
4 _____
5 _____
6 _____
7 _____
8 _____
9 _____
10 _____

Score ____

Test 14

1 _____
2 _____
3 _____
4 _____
5 _____
6 _____
7 _____
8 _____
9 _____
10 _____

Score ____

Test 15

1 _____
2 _____
3 _____
4 _____
5 _____
6 _____
7 _____
8 _____
9 _____
10 _____

Score ____

Test 16

1 _____
2 _____
3 _____
4 _____
5 _____
6 _____
7 _____
8 _____
9 _____
10 _____

Score ____

Test 17

1 _____
2 _____
3 _____
4 _____
5 _____
6 _____
7 _____
8 _____
9 _____
10 _____

Score ____

Test 18

1 _____
2 _____
3 _____
4 _____
5 _____
6 _____
7 _____
8 _____
9 _____
10 _____

Score ____

Test 19

1 _____
2 _____
3 _____
4 _____
5 _____
6 _____
7 _____
8 _____
9 _____
10 _____

Score ____

Test 20

1 _____
2 _____
3 _____
4 _____
5 _____
6 _____
7 _____
8 _____
9 _____
10 _____

Score ____

Test 21

1 _____

2 _____

3 _____

4 _____

5 _____

6 _____

7 _____

8 _____

9 _____

10 _____

Score ____

Test 22

1 _____

2 _____

3 _____

4 _____

5 _____

6 _____

7 _____

8 _____

9 _____

10 _____

Score ____

Test 23

1 _____

2 _____

3 _____

4 _____

5 _____

6 _____

7 _____

8 _____

9 _____

10 _____

Score ____

Test 24

1 _____

2 _____

3 _____

4 _____

5 _____

6 _____

7 _____

8 _____

9 _____

10 _____

Score ____

Test 25

1 _____

2 _____

3 _____

4 _____

5 _____

6 _____

7 _____

8 _____

9 _____

10 _____

Score ____

Test 26

1 _____

2 _____

3 _____

4 _____

5 _____

6 _____

7 _____

8 _____

9 _____

10 _____

Score ____

Test 27

1 _____

2 _____

3 _____

4 _____

5 _____

6 _____

7 _____

8 _____

9 _____

10 _____

Score ____

Test 28

1 _____

2 _____

3 _____

4 _____

5 _____

6 _____

7 _____

8 _____

9 _____

10 _____

Score ____

Test 29

1 _____
2 _____
3 _____
4 _____
5 _____
6 _____
7 _____
8 _____
9 _____
10 _____

Score ____

Test 30

1 _____
2 _____
3 _____
4 _____
5 _____
6 _____
7 _____
8 _____
9 _____
10 _____

Score ____

Test 31

1 _____
2 _____
3 _____
4 _____
5 _____
6 _____
7 _____
8 _____
9 _____
10 _____

Score ____